STOP

OVERTHINKING
and GET YOUR
ACT TOGETHER

13 Tips to Calm Your Anxious Mind,
Reduce Stress, Increase Productivity,
and Find Happiness

Lara J. Noble

Table of Contents

Introduction

Do you often find yourself replaying past events in your head or imagining how a future scenario could go wrong for long periods of time? Do you find it difficult to pull yourself out of these negative thought cycles? Does this type of thinking cause you to feel anxious or stressed? Do you find it difficult to concentrate on anything else while these nagging thoughts are at the front of your mind? If any of this rings true to you, you might be overthinking.

There are a lot of misconceptions about overthinking. Many people believe that overthinking is a good thing. The logic here is that the more you overthink, the more prepared you will be for any situation. This is not the case. In fact, overthinking is not logical thinking because it is fueled by stress. It will actually lead you to focus on all the wrong things, thus getting you nowhere. On top of this, the more you overthink, the less you are able to take action.

Another common misconception about overthinking is that no one else does it or that there is something wrong with you if you do. The truth is, everyone overthinks at least sometimes, and a lot of people overthink often. It's not something that we talk about enough because there can be a certain level of shame associated with it. However, this shame comes from the false belief that overthinking is not normal. If you spend a lot of time overthinking, you are not alone. Remembering this can help you push past any shame you may be carrying and redirect your energy on your desire to push past overthinking.

Because of its negative connotations, many people think that overthinking only affects people with anxiety or depression. This is not true because, again, everyone overthinks. However, anxiety and depression are related to overthinking—but overthinking does not only come from these mental health issues. In other words, anxiety and depression is not the direct cause of overthinking. Rather, it is more of a bidirectional relationship. People who are already suffering from anxiety or depression may overthink due to certain thought patterns that are fueled by these symptoms, and overthinking can also cause people to develop mental health issues like anxiety or depression.

Overthinking can also create a false sense of comfort because while you are overthinking, you are not actually dealing with the problem at hand. Overthinking is just a distraction that gets in the way of your ability to take action. Because of this, it creates much more stress in the long run. The more you remain in an overthinking headspace, the more you are fueling feelings of stress, and the more stress you feel about the topic you are overthinking, the more you will feel as though you have to keep thinking about it. This creates a vicious cycle that can be challenging to break out of. However, you will soon learn all the tools you need to break this cycle, start living in the moment, and focus on your priorities.

Overthinking may be affecting you more than you realize. Once you are used to overthinking, it can be difficult to recognize when you are overthinking versus when you are thinking things through in a healthy way. It has a direct and negative impact on your productivity and well-being. Since overthinking is both all-consuming and negative, it takes a toll on your ability to do anything else, whether it be work, social interactions, or self-care.

However, the more you know about overthinking, the easier it will become to notice when you are engaging in overthinking, and then you can start to take steps to address the issue. Once you commit to managing overthinking, you will be able to truly focus on your goals and take charge of your life.

CHAPTER 1

Understanding Overthinking

Overthinking is when you think about one thing for a long-period of time without being able to focus on anything else. This often creates more problems than it solves, despite the belief you may have that you need to keep thinking about the topic at hand.

The truth is, we all overthink from time to time. However, it is the ability to recognize when you are overthinking and then draw yourself out of this state-of-mind that will ultimately break your habit of overthinking.

There are several reasons why people overthink. When there is a problem at hand, it may seem logical to go over all the different ways that the situation could play out; however, this can easily lead to overthinking, which will get in the way of your ability to actually do anything to alleviate the problem. Some common causes of overthinking include

- stress
- perfectionism

- low self-esteem
- self-doubt
- not being solution-oriented or not wanting to take action to solve a problem
- repetitive thought cycles
- feeling like your brain just won't relax

Overthinking is also commonly linked to conditions such as anxiety, depression, post-traumatic stress disorder (PTSD), substance use disorders, and eating disorders.

Overthinking is a vicious cycle. Once you begin to overthink something, you may start to believe that continuing to think about it is the only way to work through it. Because of this, you may not even realize you are overthinking. The more you overthink the issue, the more value you are assigning it, which makes it even more difficult to let it go. In reality, the time spent overthinking could be time better spent taking action.

Some common signs that you may be overthinking include the following:

- difficulty shifting your thinking
- persistent negativity in your thinking
- feeling consumed by thoughts about things that you do not have control over
- mental or physical exhaustion
- persistent feelings of stress, worry, or anxiety
- difficulty relaxing

- getting stuck in thought loops or thinking about a past event over and over
- doubting yourself or questioning your past decisions
- jumping to the worst possible outcomes of situations

Overthinking takes a major toll on both your mental and physical health. You may find yourself suffering from mental exhaustion—this is a major side effect that comes from overthinking, and one that can get in the way of your motivation and confidence to take action. As a result, you will get stuck overthinking about a situation when you could be taking action to effectively change the situation.

Negative Self-Talk

Negative self-talk happens when intrusive thoughts start to seep into your mind. They can pop out from seemingly nowhere, and they can really have a strong effect on your mood, self-esteem, and behavior. You may be going about your day when, all of a sudden, a negative thought, such as *I'm unlovable, I look horrible today,* or *I'm not as good as this other person,* springs up in your mind. These thoughts can be quite jarring, and because of this, they are often difficult to ignore. As a result, you may begin to get wrapped up in an overthinking cycle that revolves around this negative thought. This then becomes negative self-talk.

The more space negative self-talk occupies in your mind, the harder it becomes to focus on anything else, and the worse you will feel, both mentally and physically. Negative self-talk can lead to a myriad of mental health issues and can also impact your physical health. For example, this chatter can feel so loud in your mind that you may have difficulty sleeping or relaxing throughout your day. As a result, you may develop long-term issues such as chronic insomnia or chronic muscle pain from all the tension you're holding in your body.

Some common patterns of negative self-talk include the following:

- being too hard on yourself when you experience setbacks or make mistakes
- setting unrealistic expectations
- comparing yourself to others who seem to have "more" (more money, higher-status jobs, larger social media following, etc.)

There are a number of different types of negative self-talk. Being able to identify and name the types of thought patterns you are experiencing and recognize that these thought patterns are manifesting through negative self-talk will help you separate yourself from these intrusive thoughts and break you out of an overthinking cycle.

Catastrophizing

If you catch yourself spending a lot of time thinking about the past or the future, you may be catastrophizing. This is when you focus only on the negatives of a situation. A lot of the time, this type of thinking is highly unrealistic; however, the more time you spend thinking in this way, the more real these negative potential outcomes become for you. For example, let's say you have a job interview coming up. It's not your dream job, but it is a job that you believe can help get you to where you eventually want to be career-wise. If you begin to overthink about the future, you may convince yourself that if you don't nail this job interview, you will not get the job, and then no one will want to hire you, and then you will never be able to work your way up to the job you want, and your career goals will never come to fruition.

This is catastrophizing. You are taking a future event and overthinking about the worst possible outcome, even though this imagined chain of events is highly unlikely. What's worse is that, in doing so, you are putting so much pressure on yourself to perform well in this upcoming job interview that you are setting yourself up for failure; you likely will not do your best in the interview if you go into it with heightened levels of stress that don't need to be there in the first place.

Catastrophizing can also come from overthinking about the past. This is another common way that people tend to overthink. When you catastrophize about the past, you take an event that has already happened and convince yourself that it was a negative event, regardless of whether or not it actually was. For example, let's say you were called into your boss' office earlier this morning. Maybe all your boss wanted was to have a quick chat with you about a project you're working on. The meeting was short and went smoothly. However, the more you think about it, the more you begin to wonder how the things you said in the meeting sounded. Thoughts such as, *I bet that thing I said sounded so stupid* or *Why did my boss ask me that? I bet she's questioning my decision-making,* can start to creep in and overtake you.

Overthinking in this way will deteriorate your confidence, distort your perspective on situations, and negatively impact the way you make decisions in the present. The worst part is, the more time you spend catastrophizing, the harder it will become to break out of this cycle.

Overthinking or catastrophizing about the future or the past will prevent you from living in the moment, which will ultimately get in the way of your ability to make choices and take action to get what you need and want to get done. All that catastrophizing accomplishes is leading you to obsess over worst-case scenarios, and this serves no one.

In reality, you don't really have control over the past or the future. While you can use the past to learn and grow, you can't actually change the way that past events played out because they have already happened. Similarly, while you can make present-moment decisions that impact your future, you don't have full control over future events. Since they have not happened yet, you don't truly know how future events will play out. There are many factors that may play a role in the outcome of a future event that are outside of your control. The best time to focus on is the future because it is the only time that you truly have control over. This allows you to not only live in the moment but also take action that impacts you in the most positive way.

Overgeneralizing

Overgeneralizing tends to happen when you have one negative past event that you haven't been able to shake. The outcome of this particular event plays over and over in your mind and affects the way you make decisions in the present. You come to expect this one outcome to be the overarching rule for how all similar future events will play out.

For example, maybe you were in a long-term relationship, and it ended. You convince yourself that every relationship you have from now on will only lead to heartbreak. As a result, you avoid dating altogether because you don't want to be heartbroken again.

The truth is, you may enter another relationship that ends, but you also may find the person you want to spend the rest of your life with. There is really no way of knowing how this type of future event will play out in the end. However, when you overgeneralize, you convince yourself that you do know for certain how it will play out and that it will play out badly for you.

Overgeneralizing tends to lead to quite black-and-white thinking. Every situation has its own nuances, and so every situation has possibilities for all different types of outcomes. However, black-and-white thinking and overgeneralizing pushes away all these different possibilities, and you are only able to focus on the worst possible outcome. This will prevent you from taking any action and doing the things you want because it is a fear-based reaction.

It also prevents you from seeing the good in situations that you interpret as totally bad. Even if your relationship ended and you were heartbroken, there were likely a lot of positives that you gained from your experiences while in that relationship. However, all these positives go away when you only focus on the one negative outcome that you experienced.

Filtering

Filtering is when you dwell only on negatives while filtering out the positives of any given scenario. This leaves you only with negativity because it pushes away any positivity that life throws your way. Filtering often occurs in people who tend to take criticism poorly or in people who have a negative or cynical outlook on life.

If criticism does not come easily for you, even if you have had a good day where everything has worked out how you wanted it to and all of your social interactions have been pleasant, one negative thing may be able to ruin it all for you. For example, if you've had an excellent day, and then your coworker makes a comment about how you haven't been completing your work quickly enough, this thought can potentially hold the power to stick with you for the rest of the day. You may get stuck overthinking your coworker's words for hours and actually forget all the positive things that happened that day.

By dwelling on the one negative that occurred that day, you are filtering out all the positives that you could instead be focusing on. As a result, you likely will get caught up in negative self-talk that stems from your coworker's words.

If you have a negative outlook on life, you are also more likely to find negative aspects of situations and then use these negatives to fuel negative self-talk while you filter out all the positives. Of course, no one means to do this, but it can happen for a number of reasons. Maybe when your coworker brought up your time management, they only meant it as a suggestion that you could use to improve your work. Regardless of their intent, you can interpret this scenario in a couple of different ways. When your mindset is already negative, you will likely interpret your coworker's words as being a negative criticism of you. On the other hand, if your mindset is more positive, you are more likely to interpret your coworker's words in a positive way, such as an opportunity for growth.

Here's where the first tip for moving away from overthinking comes into play. **Cultivate gratitude to focus on the positive and create a more positive mindset.** Appreciate what you have and all the opportunities life throws your way. While it's easy to get bogged down in the negatives, paying gratitude to all the positives in your life will actually open you up to receive even more positivity. Gratitude also helps you break out of overthinking by bringing you into the present moment. Being grateful for what you do have moves you away from longing for the things that you don't have or comparing yourself to others. If you are hyper-focused on the past or future, you are not able to fully appreciate your life, but making a habit of cultivating gratitude will shift your focus toward positive thinking.

The second tip to beat overthinking is to **practice self-compassion and forgive yourself for mistakes and failures.** Remember that you are human and allowed to make mistakes. In fact, by making mistakes, you are actually learning and growing. The next time you catch yourself engaging in negative self-talk, remember to be compassionate to yourself. Find the positives in the situation, and focus instead on these.

CHAPTER 2

Calming Your Anxious Mind

Having an anxious mind can feel like your brain is constantly running a mile a minute. This can lead to mental exhaustion as well as physical exhaustion, and relaxation can start to feel like a completely foreign concept. The good news is, there is a vast array of different techniques that are aimed at calming your anxious mind. Trying different techniques to see what works best for you is the first step in finally achieving the peace of mind you've been longing for.

Bringing awareness to your breathing can quickly bring you back to a calm state. When you experience anxiety, your body enters what is called the fight-or-flight state. When your body enters this state, your respiratory system prepares the body to either fight or flee the scene by increasing your heart rate and adrenaline and causing rapid, shallow breathing.

This bodily response is a product of evolution, and it has allowed humans to be better equipped to survive in the face of physical danger. However, the downside of this evolutionary marker is that sometimes our bodies respond in this way even when there is no physical threat present. Rather, when the human mind interprets a situation as anxiety-inducing, the body sometimes reacts by sending us into the fight-or-flight state.

Once in this state, you may grow even more stressed about the fact that you cannot seem to control your rapid, shallow breathing, sped-up heart rate, and potential dizziness due to improper breathing in a state of rest.

The next time this happens to you, try to take deep, steady breaths. Try counting your breaths: inhale for four seconds, then exhale for four seconds. Repeat this for about a full minute, or until you feel your heart rate slow down and your body starts to physically calm down. This focused breathing will slow down your breathing to a more normal resting state and actually bring your body out of fight-or-flight mode.

Aromatherapy is another tool that a lot of people find helpful for anxiety, and it is something that you can easily incorporate into your daily home life. Aromatherapy can be used in the form of candles, essential oils, or incense. Many people find certain natural smells soothing, such as sandalwood or lavender. However, different aromas will impact everyone differently. One smell may work wonders for one person, while doing nothing for the next. Find what you like and don't like—remember, there is no rulebook for this. Whatever works for you, works for you.

Individual preferences also are often linked with memory. Maybe your mother wore a lavender perfume, so lavender is an especially calming scent because of its familiarity. When browsing aromas, be careful of scents that are too strong. For instance, sometimes certain candles can smell too synthetic, and this can overwhelm your senses, rather than soothe them. When in doubt, trust your senses and the way that different aromas make you feel.

As we go about our days, we take in so much information, both positive and negative. This can start to overwhelm anyone, even if they are not conscious of what it is that is making them feel this way. It's important to find time during your day to shake off all the negative energy you may have picked up along the way. Meditation is a great way to reduce this type of stress by clearing your body and mind of all the information overload that you have been holding in you throughout your day. Some physical and mental benefits that meditation can bring you include the following:

- increased focus on the present moment
- increased self-awareness
- improved stress management
- heightened creativity
- improved management of negativity
- change in perspective, especially on challenging situations
- a more positive outlook
- improved tolerance and patience

Types of Meditation and Stress Management Techniques

Mindfulness

One extremely popular and effective type of meditation practice is called mindfulness. It involves increasing your awareness toward your surrounding environment and how your senses are reacting to these various external stimuli. Making these types of observations without judgment is the first step in practicing mindfulness.

In our everyday lives, we often tend to get so wrapped up in responsibilities and distractions that we do not take the time to truly notice what is going on around us or how our bodies are responding. Negative self-talk pulls us even further away from living in the moment.

With mindfulness, the goal is to center yourself back in the present moment by making observations through your senses. The more you are able to remain present, the more positive change you will be able to bring about in your life, both internally and externally.

Finding the time to practice mindfulness on a daily basis can initially seem like a daunting task; however, mindfulness practice can take as little as a few minutes, while still being highly effective in grounding you back in the present. Actually, the busier your schedule, the more you can benefit from mindfulness. It is the moments when your life feels the most chaotic when you should bring your focus back to mindfulness, as these are the moments when stress can really take over. The faster you move, the more often you will need to slow down, and mindfulness is the perfect tool to use to do so.

There are many different ways that you can start to incorporate mindfulness into your everyday life. These various techniques help relax the mind and the body in order to reduce stress.

Pay attention to your environment with all of your five senses. Making simple observations about the world around you will help slow down your mind and get you out of negative thought cycles like intrusive thoughts or negative self-talk.

Pay gratitude to the little things. Whether it be appreciating the sounds of the birds chirping outside your window in the morning or the smell of your coffee brewing, appreciating the small details of life will help center you in the present by increasing your sensory awareness.

Do a full-body scan meditation. This practice can be quick or lengthy, depending on how much time you have and what you want to achieve with it. Even if you are on your feet and have a million things going on, you can take a few seconds to check in with your body.

Starting with either your head or your toes and moving either down or up your body, pay attention to each part of your body individually. How does it feel? Are you carrying any tension in this part of your body? If so, physically release that tension by shaking it off. Imagine the tension exiting that part of your body. When you feel that tension release, move on to the next part of your body.

If you have some more time and are in a space where you are able to lie down, lie flat on your back with your palms facing upwards. Drop your shoulders down and away from your neck. Stretch out your arms and legs. Once you feel comfortable, begin your body scan.

An important part of mindfulness is to make observations without judgment. This also goes for noticing your own thoughts and emotions. We all experience negative self-talk from time to time. This is normal—it's the way that we deal with negative self-talk that can either bring us down or lift us up. The next time you notice an intrusive thought creeping into your mind, use mindfulness to positively move forward. When you become aware that you are engaging in negative self-talk, it is tempting to try to just push these thoughts away. But it can actually be more beneficial to acknowledge them. When you push these thoughts away, you are placing judgment on yourself for having these thoughts in the first place, and they will continue to resurface unless you acknowledge them.

The first step is to recognize the negative self-talk. Then, acknowledge that you had the thought and that it is just an instance of negative self-talk that is completely normal to experience. Then simply allow it to pass along. It can be helpful to visualize the thought as something like a cloud or a car. Visualize the physical representation of your negative thought moving along until you can no longer see it. This way, you are acknowledging your negative thoughts without judgment and without giving them power; you simply continue to live in the moment.

Visualization

Meditation and visualization techniques can have numerous benefits for both physical and emotional well-being. Physical and mental benefits of visualization include the following:

- improved physical abilities
- chronic pain relief
- improved management of stress and anxiety
- stronger immune system
- better sleep
- increased confidence
- improved ability to focus

Relaxation techniques such as autogenic relaxation, which focuses on visualization and physical self-awareness, can also be quite helpful in reducing stress. To begin this technique, get in a comfortable position, either lying on your back or sitting upright. Think about a peaceful place. This can either be a real place that you have been to or an imagined place.

Visualize the details of your chosen environment. If it's a beach, for example, what color is the sand? How does it feel when you run your hands through it? What do the waves sound like? What time of day is it? How does the breeze feel on your skin? Does it smell like saltwater?

The deeper you are able to dive into these types of questions that activate your senses in a calming manner, the more realistic your visualization will become, and, as a result, the more enveloped you will begin to feel in the serenity of your imagined environment.

Once you feel that your environment is clear in your mind, you can begin to focus on increasing your bodily awareness. Bring your attention to your breathing. Once in a relaxed state, your breathing will likely already be deeper and slower. Focus on how this feels and how the air that enters and exits your body relaxes and rejuvenates you. Notice your shoulders. Are you holding any tension in them? If so, drop them into a relaxed state. Focus on how each part of your body feels and how you can relax further into your physical position.

Breathwork

There are several breathing techniques that can help with relaxation and stress reduction. To begin with a simple breathing exercise, take a few deep breaths. Feel how your abdomen expands the more air you take in. Visualize the air filling your body on every inhale and rushing out from your body on every exhale. This allows you to consciously follow your breaths both physically and mentally.

Deep breathing is a simple exercise that you can do almost anywhere—you can even take a few moments to practice this while sitting at your desk at work. To begin, get into a comfortable position—you can lie on your back, sit upright in a chair, or even stand comfortably. Place one hand on your abdomen and one on your chest. Take a deep breath in through your nose. Feel your belly expand as it fills with oxygen. Slowly release your breath back out through your nose. Feel how much the hand on your abdomen moves as you continue to inhale and exhale. It should be moving more than the hand on your chest. If it is not, try to take slower, deeper breaths and focus on visualizing the oxygen you take in moving into your belly and causing it to expand with every inhalation. When you exhale, visualize sending that air from your belly back up and out through your nose. Repeat this cycle for however long you feel necessary or until you feel at peace.

Mantra-focused breathing is another popular breathwork technique that you can use to de-stress. Start by closing your eyes and getting physically comfortable, either lying down or sitting upright. Breathe deeply for a few counts as you get used to slower, deeper breaths. Imagine that there is peace and serenity in all the air surrounding you. On your next inhale, visualize this serene air entering your body and filling it up with its peace. Visualize this peaceful air spreading all the way down to the tips of your fingers and toes. As you exhale, imagine that the air you are sending out carries with it all the stress and tension you are holding in your body.

It can also be helpful to visualize the peaceful air and the stressful air as two different colors. For instance, maybe you want to visualize the positive air that you breathe into your body as light yellow and the negative air that you release from your body as deep red.

On your next inhale, choose a positive mantra that speaks to you and what you want to achieve with this meditation. This can be as simple as "I invite peace in." When you inhale the calming light yellow–colored air around you, say your mantra either in your mind or out loud. On your exhale, say either out loud or in your mind, "I release any tension and stress." Repeat these phrases on each following inhale and exhale. Continue this meditation for a few more minutes or until you feel content.

With any new meditation, it can help to set a timer. Especially if you are a beginner, keeping track of time can distract you from a meditation. Glancing at your phone to check how long you've been meditating for will pull you straight out of your meditation. On the other hand, attempting to meditate for long periods of time is also something that can get in the way of your progress. When starting out, it is best to set a goal to meditate for shorter amounts of time (five minutes, for example), more regularly (for instance, every morning). This will keep you on track to incorporate meditation into your daily routine. Meditation is like exercise: When you are first starting out, you shouldn't attempt to go for an hour-long run. Rather, it is more beneficial to progress slowly and steadily. Maintaining focus is something that will take some time to build up to.

The third tip to tackle overthinking is to **practice mindfulness daily to quiet the mind and increase self-awareness.** This will actively bring you into the present and get you away from negative self-talk and stress. The more self-aware you are, the more you are truly living in the present. Mindfulness is a tool that can change your life— just remember to use it every day. Even if you just take five minutes to slow down in a stressful situation and focus your attention on mindfulness, you can calm your mind so that when you get back to the task at hand, you are in a more relaxed, present state, and you can tackle the challenge with a fresh perspective and renewed sense of productivity.

CHAPTER 3

Reframing Negative Thoughts

There are several tools that you can use to overcome negative thought patterns. First, you will want to identify your negative thoughts. Begin to take notice of what your negative self-talk looks like. Can you notice any patterns? Maybe there are some similar thoughts that keep looping in your head. These are the ones that you want to tackle first. Choose one of these negative recurring thoughts.

Negative recurring thoughts tend to play on your vulnerabilities, and therein lies their power. However, the more you get used to reframing your vulnerabilities from a negative perspective to a positive one, the less power they will have over you. We will go over this in more detail later in this chapter.

The next step is to challenge your negative thoughts by questioning their validity. A lot of the time, negative intrusive thoughts are simply not reflective of the truth. However, it can be difficult to recognize this because of their ability to play on your vulnerabilities. Take a step back and ask yourself, "Is this thought truthful?" This will allow you to assess the thought from a more logical perspective as opposed to an emotional one.

Sometimes, however, you may find that the thought does have some truth to it. When this is the case, challenge it further. How is this thought accurate? It is best to allow yourself to be completely honest and specific.

There is also a difference between a thought being true and a thought being so prevalent in your mind that you begin to believe that it's true. It's important to take the time to really assess whether the thought is actually true or if it is just your negative thought cycles convincing you that it is true. Being able to make this distinction can be challenging, but it is important to do so.

Now you can start to reframe your thoughts. Take your negative recurring thought and see how you can reword it in a more positive light. This way, you are taking charge of your narrative instead of getting stuck in a negative thought cycle, which will only bring down your confidence.

Treat yourself with compassion. Be kind to yourself, and allow yourself to make mistakes, free from judgment. Reframing your thoughts will help with this, but it is important to keep up the work. Whenever you catch yourself getting frustrated at a mistake you made or wishing you could be more like another person, return to compassion. Remind yourself of all the things you love about yourself, and remember that you are not attached to your old negative beliefs about yourself.

Reframing your negative thoughts is essential in shifting your outlook, because while it can be tempting not to address negative thoughts altogether, it is necessary in order to combat negative self-talk. If you were to try to simply never have the negative thought, it would undoubtedly keep returning. Reframing the thought into something more positive will prevent the negativity that was associated with the initial intrusive thought from taking hold of you and making you feel worse about yourself.

Reframing Techniques

Affirmations

You can use affirmations to combat negativity—whether it be stress, overthinking, negative self-talk, thoughts, or beliefs. Positive affirmations are short statements geared toward boosting your self-esteem. They will break you out of negative thought cycles by boosting your confidence, compassion, and motivation to bring about positive change. When you repeat affirmations to yourself, you are reinforcing the thought. The more you repeat it, the more you will start to change your mindset. For example, if you tell yourself repeatedly that you can accomplish a challenging task, you will start to truly believe you can do so. This also helps get you into the habit of replacing negative self-talk with positive thoughts. Here are a few examples of positive affirmations that you can use in your own life:

27

- I am confident and capable.
- I attract positive people in my life.
- I know who I am, and I am enough.
- The positive energy around me is continuously expanding.
- I choose to be present and mindful right now.

Unless an existing affirmation speaks deeply to you, it is often best to come up with one on your own. This way, you can tailor it to best suit your needs at that particular time.

You can also try an affirmation meditation. These types of meditations are meant to inspire compassion and full self-acceptance. The first step is to come up with an affirmation that truly speaks to you in the moment. For instance, if you are feeling down about yourself because you've been having negative interactions with people throughout your day, you may want to choose an affirmation like "I free myself from criticism."

Get in a comfortable position, and close your eyes. Relax as much as possible to get rid of any tension you may be holding in your body. Take some deep breaths to center yourself, and begin to think about the love and acceptance that you have for yourself. Feel this love spread throughout your body.

Bring your attention to your breath. With every inhale, you are breathing in even more love and compassion. With every exhale, you are getting rid of all the negativity and tension you may be holding on to.

Now think about your affirmation. Repeat it to yourself, either out loud or in your head. Observe how the repetition of your affirmation makes you feel, and allow yourself to simply exist in this feeling. If you feel your mind begin to wander, draw your attention back to your affirmation, without judging your mind for wandering.

Some examples of affirmations that you can use for this exercise include the following:

1. I am worthy of love and positivity.
2. I love and accept myself fully.
3. I release what is out of my control.
4. I am constantly moving forward and growing.
5. I invite positivity and release negative energy.
6. I am in control of my mindset.
7. I am grateful for what life has given me.
8. I will continue to stand up for myself and uphold my values.
9. I am capable of great things.
10. I am surrounded by people who love and appreciate me.
11. I hold the power to pave my own journey.
12. I trust the path I am on.
13. I am right where I need to be.
14. I embrace my authentic self.
15. I release my past.
16. I forgive myself.
17. I choose to learn from my mistakes.
18. I embrace balance in my life.

19. I am resilient and can overcome any challenge.
20. I am proud of all my accomplishments.
21. I have worked hard for my success.
22. I acknowledge and respect my boundaries.
23. I surround myself with positive, loving energy.
24. I am prepared for challenges.
25. I stand by my decisions.
26. I am in control of my own happiness and choose to cultivate positivity.
27. I am becoming the best version of myself each day.
28. I can find the positives in any situation.
29. I embrace positive change.
30. I am at peace.

Cultivating Gratitude

Finding the positives in situations and making the effort to feel grateful are powerful steps in your goal to reframe your negative thinking. Pay attention to all the good things that occur in your life on a daily basis. Simply opening yourself up to notice the positives of everyday life can help you develop a more grateful mindset. In doing so, you are limiting negativity. When you focus on the positive, there is less room for negative thoughts and, as a result, less room for negative feelings. Here are some ways that you can start actively cultivating gratitude.

Start keeping a gratitude journal. Spending as little as 15 minutes at the end of every day to write down what you are grateful for or moments of positivity that you noticed throughout your day can make a huge impact on your mindset. Journaling at the same time every day will help get you into the habit of expressing gratitude every day.

Don't limit yourself to expressing gratitude only on special occasions. Gratitude can and should be expressed daily. The more you get used to the practice, the more you are opening yourself to more gratitude and more positivity.

If you want to focus specifically on reframing negative self-talk, keeping a gratitude journal where you write about your daily wins can help boost your self-confidence and reframe any potential negative thoughts to positive self-talk. Start by committing to writing down three things that you accomplished that day that you are proud of. These don't have to be major life accomplishments. In fact, keeping them simple can help reframe your thinking so that you start to see positivity in seemingly small, everyday occurrences that you may have otherwise overlooked.

Afterwards, you can also write down three goals that you want to work toward tomorrow—just make sure that you are framing everything in your journal as positives. Writing down your goals for the day will help you keep track of your progress toward these goals. This can help you to recognize and acknowledge your accomplishments, no matter how important or mundane they may seem.

When journaling about your daily wins, pay attention not only to the more obvious wins, such as completing tasks for work, but also the wins that may not be as tangible. For example, maybe today you remembered to practice mindfulness when you noticed yourself feeling stressed.

This is a huge win and something you should express gratitude for because it indicates a positive change in your mindset.

There are so many things to be grateful for—it's just a matter of paying attention. The more you are able to track your progress and express gratitude, the more primed your thinking will become to pick up on these sources of positivity.

Cultivating gratitude encourages positive progress. Choosing to be grateful helps you strengthen your self-confidence and your determination to keep learning and growing because you are celebrating your progress at every step of the way.

Make a conscious choice when you wake up every day to appreciate yourself, those around you, and what life has to offer. Committing to this goal every morning will help you keep gratitude on your mind throughout your day. Keep reminding yourself to do so if you start to feel yourself falling off. This is especially important when you start to feel negative thoughts or emotions creep in. Reminding yourself to find the positives in your given circumstance can have the power to reframe your negative mindset and change your whole day.

Live in the moment. When you start to get caught up in negative thought cycles, it is usually because you are overthinking something that either happened in the past or something that might happen in the future. Gently bring yourself back to the present by noticing sensory details about your environment. This will help refocus you on what you are thankful for right now.

Focus on the people you love. A lot of the time, we take people for granted. Even if we appreciate them, we tend not to express this to them. You might fear sounding overly sentimental or cheesy. However, the truth is, people appreciate feeling appreciated—especially when they are important people in your life. Don't be afraid to tell your loved ones how much they matter to you. Take the time to really consider what makes someone special to you. The more specific you can get, the more personalized and meaningful the sentiment becomes.

Cognitive Restructuring

Cognitive behavioral therapy (CBT) is a therapeutic method used to treat psychological concerns that centers around identifying and reframing thought and behavioral patterns. For example, a patient may believe that consuming alcohol is the only way for them to numb the emotional pain of grief. Through CBT, the patient will learn how to shift their perspective surrounding this false belief. In doing so, they will recognize that alcohol actually perpetuates their feelings of grief and that suppressing their emotions prevents them from moving forward.

Cognitive restructuring is one technique that is used as part of CBT. This technique works by helping you recognize any thought patterns or false beliefs that may be holding you back (Clark, 2014).

According to psychologist JoaquínSelva (2018), The ABCDE model, which is an updated version of Albert Ellis' original ABC model, outlines the factors behind negative thought patterns. Ellis developed the ABC model as a tool to assist with a therapeutic method known as rational-emotive behavior therapy (REBT). In the updated model, ABCDE stands for the following:

- A: Activating event—an event that triggers negative thoughts or emotions
- B: Beliefs—the beliefs or thoughts about the activating event
- C: Consequences—the emotional and behavioral consequences of the beliefs
- D: Dispute—challenging and disputing the negative beliefs
- E: Effect—the effect of disputing the negative beliefs, leading to a change in emotions and behaviors

When used for cognitive restructuring, this model allows patients a method by which to identify thought patterns. From here, they are able to reconstruct these thought patterns into positives, which then has a positive effect on their behaviors and emotions (Selva, 2018).

Identify and challenge negative thought patterns and self-talk to reframe your thinking. This is the fourth tip to moving forward from overthinking. The more you get used to recognizing negative self-talk, the more you will be able to shift your thinking before these negative thoughts take over.

CHAPTER 4

Overcoming Perfectionism

While perfectionism certainly has its benefits, it can also carry a lot of negativity when taken too far. For instance, perfectionism often leads to procrastination because of the overwhelming need to produce a perfect product. The high levels of stress surrounding the need to be perfect and the unrealistic expectations you can set for yourself to achieve perfection can stand in the way of you actually doing whatever it is you want to get done. This can eventually lead to a pattern of refusing to do anything unless it is something that you know you will succeed in; this type of behavior can clearly become incredibly limiting and frustrating. Some other negative outcomes that perfectionism often leads to include

- fear of confronting challenges
- all-or-nothing thinking
- limited creativity
- constant comparisons to others

It can also lead to several mental health issues such as

- depression
- anxiety
- social anxiety
- agoraphobia
- self-harm

When making goals, it is important that you are setting challenging yet realistically achievable expectations for yourself. Setting expectations for yourself will allow you to more clearly be able to visualize your desired result. In this way, setting expectations is the first step in succeeding with your long-term goals, as long as they remain realistic. Otherwise, you will be setting yourself up for disappointment when you are not able to live up to these expectations. Remember that you are human, and allow yourself the freedom for ups and downs on your journey. You won't (and shouldn't) be perfect all the time—slipups and mistakes are simply part of reality, so it is best to plan realistically for them.

When setting realistic goals, it's crucial not to compare yourself to others. Everyone has different sets of abilities, strengths, and limitations. A goal that may be realistic for one person may not be realistic for someone else, and it doesn't have to be. However, it is usually best to simply stay away from comparison whenever possible so that you can avoid feelings of frustration and insecurity that may arise from comparing yourself to others.

Perhaps the most important factor when setting a goal is your honest belief that you can achieve it. If you don't realistically believe that a goal is achievable for you, it is not the time to set that goal for yourself. You may be able to set that goal sometime in the future, but unless you trust that it is achievable at the moment you set the goal, it isn't truly a goal—it is a fantasy.

Setting achievable goals allows you to accomplish more goals faster. The more goals you accomplish, the more you will boost your self-confidence, and the more at ease you will become setting expectations, working toward goals, and seeing positive change manifest in your life.

Strategies to Combat Perfectionism

Write Down Your Goals

Writing down your goals is a simple yet highly effective technique that can help you combat perfectionism. By writing down your goal, you are getting it out of your head and into the physical world in a tangible way. The act of writing something down helps solidify that goal in your memory and emphasizes its significance.

By writing down a goal, you can begin to analyze what you want to achieve and how you want to achieve it. This is a great way to start managing your expectations and work toward your desired outcome.

It also gives your goals more organization. Instead of trying to keep track of your various goals and the progress you're making with each of these goals in your head, writing them down allows you to see and keep track of them more clearly.

Start by setting a few goals. Don't give yourself a massive list of every goal you can think of. By having a more succinct list, you are able to dedicate more attention to accomplishing the tasks at hand. This way, you will be able to prioritize what you want in life and the steps you will take to get there. You can also set time frames for each of your goals as a way to track them. Setting smaller, achievable goals will accumulate over time so that you can accomplish larger, more complex goals in a more productive and manageable way.

The SMART goal system was introduced by George Doran in 1981. The SMART acronym stands for specific, measurable, attainable, relevant, and time-oriented. According to this model, when setting goals, you should make sure that they adhere to the qualifications outlined in the acronym (Linscott, 2023). When you set a goal, write it down and go through the following checklist:

- Is it clear and specific enough that there is no room for ambiguity?
- Is it measurable in a way that you can track your progress when working toward the goal and clearly know when you have reached it?
- Is it something that you believe you can achieve?
- Is it realistically something that feels within reach?
- Is it something that can be achieved within a certain time-frame?

A majority of the goals that you set for yourself should be able to check all five boxes; however, certain goals do not necessarily need all five. For instance, certain goals will not be measurable in a concrete way.

Writing this out will help you analyze each of your goals and make adjustments when needed.

Release the Need to Control

Letting go of control can feel scary. Being in control of a situation may feel naturally comforting to you because when you are in control, you feel like the outcomes of events will go your way. However, the desire to control everything in your life can easily grow out of control to the point where it stands in your way. When this desire takes over, you may desperately try to regain control over every little thing—even the things that you cannot realistically have control over. You may also begin to avoid certain activities that you don't know how to control. Letting go of control means embracing the unknown. This will take some time to get used to because many people harbor deep fears of the unknown—especially people with perfectionist tendencies.

If you know the outcome of everything you do, you are severely limiting your potential. Getting outside of your comfort zone is the only way to grow. When you remain locked in your comfort zone, you are not challenging yourself or learning from new opportunities and experiences. You may notice that when you only do things that you have comfortable control over, you never truly feel satisfied. This is because these experiences are no longer stimulating for you. You already know how they are going to play out.

In reality, the only thing that you truly have full control over is your own outlook. Accepting this idea will bring you a strengthened sense of peace because you will release the idea that everything that happens in your life is fully your own responsibility. There are many, many external factors that all play a role in the outcomes of events in your life. Trying to control all of these outcomes is not only exhausting, but also unrealistic. Instead, channel your energy onto the way you want to respond to these outcomes. Changing your mindset is the most influential way to bring about positive change.

There is also an incorrect connotation between control and strength. Likewise, society tends to associate a surrender of control with weakness. In reality, this is simply not the case. Accepting that you do not have to control everything actually requires a great deal of strength, bravery, and self-awareness.

Embrace Imperfection

Embracing and learning from mistakes can lead to many different benefits. This change in mindset opens you up to take more risks and push past your comfort zone, which can lead to immense personal growth as well as build your critical thinking and problem-solving skills. When you embrace imperfection and choose to learn from mistakes, you are becoming the best and truest version of yourself, and you are not held back by fear. Learning from mistakes leads you to reflect on yourself in specific ways, whether it be your values, your goals, your strengths, your progress and growth, or the areas you wish to improve. Because of this, embracing failure actually sets you up for success in the long run. It allows you to make adjustments to better approach your goals and keep moving forward with your newfound knowledge and experience.

It's always important to remind yourself that everyone makes mistakes. It is part of being human. The more frustrated you get with yourself over making a mistake, the more you are just getting in your own way. In order to be able to move on from mistakes, you have to forgive yourself for making them. But this can be easier said than done. So how do you release the frustration you may feel for making a mistake so that you are able to move forward? It all comes down to perspective.

Instead of viewing mistakes as failures, think of them as learning opportunities. Mistakes offer you the unique opportunity to learn the most. Think of where you would be without mistakes. Chances are, you would know a lot less than you do now. Mistakes allow you to grow. Shifting your perspective in this way will open you up to receive more positives from your mistakes. You will also feel more ready to forgive yourself as opposed to wishing you could change your past actions.

Reframe how you view imperfections. Maybe you have a personality trait that you view as negative. This is something you wish you could change about yourself. Maybe you see other people who seem to be doing a million things on any given day, and you wish you could be more like them in this way, but you just can't seem to get as much done in a day as these other people, no matter how hard you try. Instead of viewing this part of yourself as a negative, think about what is positive about it. Maybe you really dive deep into what you're doing, whether it be getting your work done or spending time with your family. When you do something, you really commit to fully doing it. This is why you aren't able to do as many things as other people who prefer to do many different things but not commit as fully to them as you would.

By reframing your thinking in this way, you move from a negative thought, *I can't get very many things done*, to a positive thought, *I engage fully in everything I do.* This also helps you embrace your individuality and move away from comparing yourself to others. Remember that everyone is different—it's not a matter of being better or worse than someone else.

By embracing the imperfections that make you the person you are, you are also opening up room for personal growth. It can help to frame these opportunities in terms of goals. Let's use embracing imperfections as your target goal. In this case, your perfectionism would be the trait that you want to use for personal growth. Start by releasing all the negative connotations you may be holding toward your perfectionism. Rather than a weakness, it is an area where you can grow and learn from. When you view a personality trait as a weakness, you are closing yourself off to change because you are more likely to try to avoid doing things to challenge this trait instead of actively working to improve this area.

Practice Positive Self-Talk

Take note of the way you talk to yourself. If your thoughts tend to be more negative toward yourself, odds are these negative thoughts are getting in the way of your ability to work toward your goals.

Self-talk has a powerful effect on your mood. Because of this, it can either build you up and set you up for success, or it can bring you down and set you up for failure. Practicing regular positive self-talk has the power to boost you up and motivate you toward your goals. The more confidence you are able to build within yourself, the easier working toward your goals will become because you are no longer fighting against feelings of self-doubt that stand in the way of you taking effective action.

If you notice that you are regularly engaging in negative self-talk, try to rephrase your self-talk as a positive. Changing the narrative of the way you think about yourself takes time, but the more you get used to it, the more you will start to see how positive self-talk reflects not only in your outlook but also in your actions.

This brings us to the fifth tip for overcoming overthinking. **Embrace imperfection and let go of the need for control to overcome perfectionism.** If you are constantly waiting for things to become perfect, you will never get anything done. Recognizing and actually appreciating imperfection will help you release the stress that may be surrounding certain tasks, activities, or goals. By doing this, you limit the space for overthinking because you are able to focus on the present and accept things for what they are, without getting stuck thinking about how you can achieve perfection.

CHAPTER 5

Prioritizing Tasks and Time Management

Time management techniques can help you prioritize your tasks and actively work toward your goals. First, you will want to identify your goals. Writing them down can help you visualize and organize them by priority level. Refer back to the SMART model to assess the achievability of your goals and alter them if need be.

Pay attention to how you spend your time. Take some time with this. Tracking the way you spend your time for one day will not necessarily be reflective of your typical day. If you only pay attention on one day, you are also more likely to be hyper-aware or self-conscious of what you are doing with your time and, thus, are not as likely to go about your day as you normally would. Once you begin to notice how your time is largely being spent, you will become more aware of areas where you can improve your time management. For instance, if you work from home and put on a 45-minute long episode of television every time you eat lunch, you may find that this is ultimately too long of a break for you and that it is difficult to refocus on your tasks when you do get back to work. Write down any observations that stand out to you.

Prioritize what you need to get done. It can also be helpful to write this out. Start by writing down everything you want to accomplish within a certain time frame. Especially when starting out, it can be most useful to take this day-by-day. Then, prioritize the tasks that are most important to you to get done. Put the tasks that hold the most significance at the top of your list. This will allow you to focus on one thing at a time and ensure that you accomplish what is most important to you.

A lot of the time, we can distract ourselves with tasks that, while on our to-do-list, are not as important as other tasks that we need to get done but that we may be procrastinating. For example, when I was in college and had a big paper or project due, I would often clean my entire apartment instead of working on my schoolwork. The anxiety surrounding the importance of the assignment, combined with my perfectionism, resulted in me procrastinating getting the assignment done, even though it was the task I should have been prioritizing. By cleaning my apartment, I still felt like I was being productive while also putting off the task that I actually held immediate importance. If you find yourself in this pattern of behavior, refer back to your prioritized list. This will help you stay on track and change your mindset surrounding your priorities and time management.

When making your prioritized list, it can help to think of your tasks in terms of importance and urgency. Tasks with higher urgency and importance will be at the top of your list, tasks that are important but not urgent will come next, tasks that are urgent but not important will follow, and at the bottom of your list will be tasks that are neither important nor urgent (most of the time, you can disregard these tasks, or only get to them if you have completed all other tasks). For example, let's say you have the following tasks:

- picking up your child from school
- meal prep
- returning a missed call from a friend
- watching YouTube videos

These tasks should be attended to in this order. Picking up your child from school is both urgent and important. You have also made a goal to improve your health, so meal prep is something that is important to you but does not have as much urgency. While returning a missed phone call from a friend may seem urgent, as she will be expecting a call within a certain time frame, it does not have a high level of importance since she has just called to chat. Watching YouTube videos is neither important nor urgent because this is a distractor that can get in the way of you completing your other tasks.

Making lists like these is part of planning ahead, which is an important step in learning how to manage your time. Thinking ahead and planning out how to best go about spending your time will make a huge difference in your time management skills. Setting daily goals for yourself allows you to focus on your priorities instead of getting distracted by in-the-moment stressors and chaos. Planning ahead is best done either the night before or right after you wake up. This way, you have a solid game plan for your daily tasks without having wasted any time.

Set time limits. This will ensure that you do not get burned out or waste time on tasks that can burn through your whole day. For instance, going through emails is something that can take up your whole day if you don't set time limits. Allotting a certain amount of time to focus on emails will keep you on schedule to complete your higher priority tasks. Also, this way you will be able to focus your full attention on answering emails, and when you're done, you can focus your full attention on the next task. On the other hand, if you periodically check your emails throughout the day without paying attention to time, it will be harder to return your attention to the task you are meant to be focusing your full attention on.

Taking periodic breaks throughout your day—especially if you are working on one task for a longer period of time— will actually help boost your overall productivity. A lot of the time, when we are behind on work, it can feel like there is simply no time for even a quick break. Instead, it can be tempting to keep working until we are totally burned out.

However, when you allow yourself short, regular breaks, you are able to maintain a higher level of productivity than if you try to force yourself to work for hours on end until you finish.

How exactly should you be planning out your breaks? This can be tricky since different break techniques work for different people, but here are a few options that tend to be effective:

- 50 minutes of work followed by 10 minutes of break time
- 30 minutes of work followed by 5 minutes of break time
- 1 hour of work followed by 15 minutes of break time, then 2 hours of work followed by 30 minutes of break time
- 25 minutes of work followed by 5 minutes of break time, repeat this four times, then begin to take 15-30-minute breaks when you reach your break time

Experiment with different break schedules to see what best suits you. Once you figure out a method that works well for you, you will be able to adopt this schedule into your daily life for more productive results. Pay attention to your mental state and how clearheaded and motivated you are when you return to work from a break.

Learn to say no. This can be incredibly difficult for some people—especially those who are used to overworking themselves or wanting to please others. However, learning how to say no is an important step in prioritizing your tasks and managing your time while also taking care of yourself. When you say yes to everything that is asked of you, you will not possibly be able to get everything done to your best ability. As a result, all of your work will suffer, and instead of feeling satisfied and proud after finishing your work, you will feel drained and disappointed.

When you need to finish a task that is important and urgent, it is often better to focus on this task alone and say no to incoming requests than to take on additional tasks and feel the work pile up without being able to properly attend to your prioritized list. Remember that a prioritized list will not be effective if it is too cluttered.

Get organized. We've talked about how to organize your tasks and time management, but it is also important to organize your physical space. When your workspace is cluttered, you can start to feel overwhelmed, which will lead to more stress in your work. Eliminating clutter boosts productivity because a clear space leads to a clear mind, while, on the other hand, a cluttered space leads to a cluttered mind. A clutter-free environment will best support your productivity and mental organization. As a result, living clutter-free promotes stress relief, giving you more time and energy to focus on your priorities.

If you work from home, it can be especially helpful to establish a specific area for your work where you eliminate all outside distractions. This can mean leaving your phone in another room, not having access to the television, or establishing that family members should not disturb you while you are working here, unless it is an emergency. Make sure that this space only includes physical elements that are helpful for your productivity. For instance, you may be someone who benefits from having Post-it notes on your desk to remind you when to take a break or that have inspirational messages. You may like to keep a small plant or scented candle on your desk because it makes you feel peaceful and helps keep you centered. However you want to decorate your workspace make sure it has a specific purpose for being there or else it is just clutter.

Timeboxing is another technique used for time management and achieving goals. With this technique, you set what are called timeboxes, which represent a time frame and a goal. You start by setting a time frame for your first timebox. You then assign one task for this timebox. The goal here is to accomplish this task within its accompanying time frame. When first starting out with this technique, it is best to only create a few timeboxes so as to avoid unintentionally overwhelming yourself.

If you do not reach the end of a task before your allocated time runs out, simply move on to your next timebox. This timebox can represent break time. For example, let's say your first timebox is two hours focused on creating a work presentation. At the end of the two hours, you are not quite done creating your presentation. However, your next time box is 15 minutes of break time. This works out well because after working on your presentation for two hours, you likely will benefit the most from taking a break. So at this point you will take your break and reflect on what you were able to accomplish. It is often more beneficial to stick to your timeboxes—especially when taking breaks—than to try to force yourself to keep working on one task. Timeboxing allows you to move on from a task and shift your focus onto something new, which a lot of people may find helpful. You can always return to your initial task if you need to complete it, but breaking up the time you spend working on a single task can actually boost productivity and prevent burnout.

Breaking Down Tasks

If a task is complex and requires many different steps, it is best to break it down into bite-sized pieces. This way, you can focus on completing these individual steps, one at a time. Before you break down a complex task, look at the big picture. This will help you visualize what you want the end result to look like, and it will give you something to refer back to if you start feeling stuck at any point during the process. Once you understand the goal, you can look at the different steps that you need to accomplish to reach it. What are the different tasks that you need to complete? What order do you need to complete these tasks in? Writing this down will help you stay organized and on track. Using a time management strategy that works for you, such as timeboxing, lay out everything that you need to get done within a certain time frame. When you are planning out how to best utilize your time, allow some extra time toward the end of every step for reflection. This will allow you to review what you have accomplished, feel proud of your work, and have space to shift your focus onto your next task.

It is also important to allow for some extra time in your schedule that is not necessarily planned. As you probably know, things change! It's one thing to plan out every minute of your day and another thing entirely to actually be able to follow through with this type of overly meticulous schedule. When unexpected changes occur, you will feel even more stressed because you will feel like you are behind the schedule that you set for yourself. To avoid this, it is best to accept that there will be unexpected occurrences on any given day. Accepting this will allow you to plan for it by setting aside time between tasks so that you have a little wiggle room. It will also allow you to take on these unexpected challenges with confidence instead of stress.

When you plan ahead and make a manageable schedule for yourself by breaking down large goals into individual tasks that are easier to digest, you reduce the risk of overthinking. When you jump right into a goal without thinking first about how to tackle it, you will feel more stressed and frustrated because you do not have a solid plan of action. It can sometimes be tempting—especially when you have a complex task that you need to get done more urgently—to just get straight to work. This can often seem like the best way to get something done quickly because you eliminate the time spent mapping out a plan. However, in the long run, going in without a plan will cause you to hit more roadblocks and feel less confident (and then feel less motivated to continue as a result), which will actually slow you down.

This is especially true if you are a perfectionist. Even if you are working on overcoming your perfectionism, don't set yourself up to fall into perfectionist traps. Likewise, don't try to tackle goals without any kind of plan. Set yourself up for success, both with your daily tasks and your longer-term goal of overcoming perfectionism.

When setting your daily goals, it can be helpful to ask why you need to get these tasks done. This will help you organize your priorities, as oftentimes a certain task may initially seem of high importance but when you ask yourself why it is a priority, it becomes clear that it is not as important as you had initially thought. These types of tasks are time wasters. Once you realize that something is a time waster, you gain the power to ignore it, allowing you to focus on the goals that are important to you.

If a task is urgent but not important and does not require as much focus as your more important or complex goals, you can work on it when your concentration is not at a peak. For example, I find that I work best in the mornings while I'm having my coffee. Because of this, I do my most important tasks during this time because I am at my productive peak. On the other hand, in the evenings, my mental energy tends to decline a little. This is why I save the tasks that are less important to me for the evenings—I do not need to be dedicating my peak performance to these tasks, so I know not to waste my peak hours on them. Recognizing when you tend to feel the most productive is an important step in managing how you spend your time.

Tip number six is to **prioritize tasks and manage your time effectively to reduce stress and increase productivity.** Time management plays a huge role in your overall mental health. Without it, you will feel stressed, frustrated, unproductive, and dissatisfied. However, there are different tools that you can use to help you effectively manage your time. In doing so, you will see your productivity rise, giving you ample opportunity to focus on your priorities.

When you set your priorities, you make the decision to commit to what matters the most to you. This leads us to tip number seven. **Align your goals and actions with your values and purpose to find meaning and fulfillment.** This way, the goals and actions that you are spending the most time and energy on are the ones that lead to a greater sense of fulfillment and personal growth.

CHAPTER 6

Mindful Communication and Relationships

We've discussed how to incorporate mindfulness in your own life and use it to improve your mental state and self-esteem, but you can also use mindfulness in your relationships. Just as mindfulness trains you to accept and acknowledge certain thoughts that you may have without judgment, this principle also applies to interactions with others. It will help you become more of an active listener without feeling the need to place any judgment on the speaker.

You may find that many times when you're listening to someone, a lot of the information they're saying gets lost on you. Maybe you zone in and out of the conversation—not because you're being rude or don't care about what they have to say but because your focus simply wavers. It's hard to take in everything through listening without the proper tools. This is where mindful communication comes in.

Not only will mindful communication help improve your active listening skills and strengthen your relationships, but it will also help develop your empathy—one of the most important human traits.

Empathy is the cornerstone of any healthy relationship. It is what allows us to understand one another and be able to put ourselves in another person's shoes even if we have not experienced exactly what they are going through. The more empathy you have, the easier conflict management will be because of this heightened understanding. You are more willing to acknowledge and accept different perspectives because you can understand how a person may have developed these points of view. The more empathetic a person you are, the more others will feel comfortable confiding in you and expressing their authentic self. Think about how much easier life would be if everyone were able to express a little more empathy.

Empathy is the key idea behind mindful communication. When you are listening to someone, you want to make sure that you are present in the conversation—which is where the mindfulness element comes in. The more you practice mindfulness in your everyday life, the easier it will be to then apply mindfulness to other areas, such as communication and interpersonal relationships.

Mindful listening will make the other person feel seen and heard. It creates a safe space for both parties. No one wants to open up to someone who doesn't appear to be listening to what they have to say. On the other hand, when you are speaking with someone and you can tell that they are genuinely interested and present in the conversation, it makes you feel accepted and free to express what it is you want to talk about.

With mindful listening, you want to get rid of any distractions. This means putting your phone away, facing away from any distractions that may be going on in the background, and being fully present with the other person. Bringing your full attention to the present conversation will also help prevent your mind from wandering to other personal distractions that may be occupying your mind, such as any conflicts you are dealing with or what you're going to have for dinner that night.

Mindful communication also includes getting involved in the conversation, not only by actively listening but also by engaging in the conversation. For example, if someone is coming to you for advice on an issue they're struggling with, asking open-ended questions is a way to help the other person talk through their issue in a guided yet free way.

Pay attention not only to what the other person is saying but also to how they are expressing themselves. Body language and tone of voice are both helpful indicators of how someone is feeling. For a number of reasons, it's often difficult to get across everything we want to say. Listening to nonverbal clues can help you fill in the gaps when it comes to what someone else is wanting to communicate to you.

Remember to breathe (and remind the other person to breathe, too, if necessary). Sometimes when you are listening to another person's problems, you can start to pick up their stress. As a result, you can begin to feel overwhelmed not because you are in their situation but because you are empathizing with their situation. Taking a moment to breathe will help keep you centered and stress-free so that you can continue to actively listen to what the other person is saying. This will also help you think before you speak. For example, if a good friend is telling you about her relationship troubles and asks you what you think, your initial response may be to say that you think she should break up with her partner. However, this will likely not be the reaction your friend needs at this moment. Instead, take a moment, breathe, and think of a gentler way to express your concern about her relationship. Breathing helps slow you down, which is important in communication—especially when discussing complicated and emotional issues. Slowing down in an instance like this can help you avoid saying something you don't mean or offending the other person.

Know when you need to find another time to talk. Everyone has moments when they simply cannot focus their attention on a conversation—especially if it's a difficult conversation to have. If you are finding it too difficult to give the other person your full attention, you may want to be honest about it and instead agree to find another time to have this discussion. It's better to openly express how you are feeling than to stop paying attention to the other person. Not engaging in a conversation helps no one—the speaker will just be talking to a brick wall, and you will not register anything they are telling you.

When you start to feel your mind wander, use your mindfulness techniques to draw your attention back to the present moment. Don't judge yourself for letting your mind wander; rather, gently bring your focus back to the speaker or to the topic at hand.

Conflict Management

Conflict management is not necessarily something you want to need to practice a lot, but it is something that is essential for moving forward. Being able to effectively manage conflict will allow you to help bring about positive change, come to understandings with others who you had a previous disagreement with, improve communication between yourself and others, and strengthen relationships.

When you are talking through an issue with someone, ensure that both parties are comfortable. Your surrounding environment can play a huge role in your level of comfort. Just as with mindful communication, it is best to avoid distractions wherever possible. This means going somewhere relatively calm and quiet and putting away your devices. Even if you are not talking to someone in person—whether it be a phone call, video chat, or via text—make sure that you are in a space, both physically and mentally, where you can devote your full attention to the conversation with this other person. Remember that conflict management can be challenging, so set yourself up for success by heading into it with a helpful environment.

Be empathetic to the other person's wishes while also keeping in mind your own wishes. If the conflict has arisen because the two of you want two different things, try to steer the conversation toward finding a compromise where both of you can benefit. Be mindful of their feelings, but don't ignore your own feelings.

Talk out the facts surrounding the source of conflict. This will help the other person understand how you view the conflict. Allowing the other person to then share their interpretation of the conflict will give you the opportunity to look at the situation from their perspective. Talking through the situation will help both parties understand the nature of the conflict. This way, both of you are better prepared to find a solution.

When you're sharing your perspective, it's important to use language that does not make the other person feel attacked.

Antagonizing language such as "You did this wrong," will only heighten the other person's defenses. Instead, try using "I" statements. For example, "I felt like I had to pick up the slack at work last week because I kept having to work overtime, and this made me feel frustrated." Be as specific as you can while maintaining this type of phrasing. This allows the other person a better opportunity to be able to put themselves in your shoes and, thus, understand where you are coming from.

Make sure the other person feels free to express themselves without judgment. You can do this by directly asking them to share their perspective on the topic at hand. Let them know that you want to understand their thoughts on the issue, and vice versa. Allow them the space to fully explain their point of view before responding. This way, they will feel free to get everything out in the open.

While engaging in conflict management, you may sometimes need to take breaks. If the conflict is complex, or emotions are running high, it's okay to voice a need to step away and return to the conversation at a later time. If the conversation is causing even more stress, a break will be necessary to center yourself so that you can work through the conflict with a clear head. Taking a break and then returning to the subject can also help you approach the issue with a fresh perspective. It's important, however, when breaking from the conversation, to establish a specific time when both parties are able to continue the conversation. Otherwise, the issue may remain unresolved for longer than needed, or you or the other person may be tempted to put it off.

Know when to ask another person to mediate. This applies if you are particularly wary about how a conversation may go or if things begin to get heated and you agree to continue the conversation at another time. However, it is essential when choosing someone to mediate that they are someone who both parties are comfortable with but who will not take sides. This person is here to help keep the conversation on track, friendly, and solution-oriented. For example, if it is a workplace conflict, asking a manager to act as this person can help create a safe space and keep the conversation professional and on track. The manager will want to help the two of you reach a compromise so that both of you can move forward.

Following up is often a great extra step to take because it shows that you care about the other person's feelings, and it can help strengthen your relationship. It is also important in assessing how well the compromise you reached is working. Thank the other person for taking the time to come to a conclusion and for being willing to come up with a compromise. Following up improves the conflict management experience as a whole so that the next time you may have a conflict with this person, it is not as difficult or uncomfortable to navigate.

Overthinking in Relationships

Overthinking can strain relationships and cause heightened levels of stress about issues that can seem like the end of the world but that are, in reality, quite minor. As you know, overthinking can cause one issue you're thinking about to quickly overpower you to the point where it's all you can think about. In a relationship, overthinking can actually create problems that were not there to begin with.

Overthinking, as previously discussed, gets in the way of you being present. This holds true for your relationships as well. When you overthink about your relationship, you are not able to live presently in that relationship. The more this goes unchecked, the more tense you will become, and the more strain this will place on your relationship. This can cause you to lash out at your partner, creating an even wider gap between the two of you. When you are not fully present, you are not able to properly assess the current situation. This will lead you to misinterpret situations in your relationship, as you begin to overthink them instead of looking at the situation with a more logical perspective.

Approaching relationships with empathy is the best way to strengthen your connection and pull yourself out of an overthinking cycle. Mindful communication and empathy go hand in hand. Empathy is required for mindful communication, and vice versa; you cannot have one without the other. So, the more you are able to practice these skills, the more growth you will see in both of these areas. Increased empathy in a relationship leads to increased compassion, understanding, and freedom to express honest feelings between partners.

In order to build your empathy, you first need to practice identifying your own emotions. Start to pay attention to how you are feeling at different times. See if you can name your emotions. Be as specific as possible, and do so without any judgment. For instance, if you are feeling jealous, acknowledge and name this feeling honestly without judging yourself for feeling this way. The more comfortable and familiar you become with your own emotional life, the more you will be able to identify the emotions of others around you and be able to put yourself in their shoes. On the other hand, if, for instance, you are never willing to acknowledge when you are feeling angry, you will not feel comfortable empathizing with someone who is feeling angry. It's not necessarily that the feeling of anger itself is foreign to you, but it's the recognition of the sentiment that you are not comfortable with yet.

Pay attention to your partner's needs. This means being open with your communication about your own needs and encouraging your partner to do the same. The more comfortable both of you feel expressing your emotional and physical needs, the easier it will be to meet these needs.

Accept your partner for who they are. Every aspect of their personality is a part of what makes them the unique individual they are. You and your partner are not going to be exactly the same, and nor should you try to be. However, this also means that they will react differently to certain situations than you would. Understanding their personality and the way that different situations affect them will help you put yourself in their shoes even when you are not actually experiencing the same emotions they are.

Actively listen when they express their emotions. This will help you understand their perspective. Even though two people may have differing perspectives, you are still able to understand the reasons behind the other person's perspective. This is important to remember when your partner is being emotionally vulnerable with you. During these moments, the more you are able to put yourself in their shoes, the more empathy you will feel toward them, and your partner will feel that empathy. Being treated empathetically will make them feel comfortable and safe, which will make them feel more open to continue to express their emotions with you moving forward, and this will strengthen your bond.

Don't ignore your own needs. Being empathetic in your relationship also requires you to stay attentive to your own well-being. Take time during the day to reflect on how you are feeling. Then, ask yourself what you need. Just as your partner feels comfortable leaning on you for support, you can also lean on your partner for emotional support. In all healthy relationships, the give-and-receive balance needs to be maintained in order for the relationship to remain two-sided.

The eighth tip for overcoming overthinking is to **develop strong communication skills to build better relationships**

and manage conflict. When you practice mindful communication, you are tapping into your empathy, which directly brings you into the present. In doing so, you are pulled out of any overthinking you may be engaging in.

CHAPTER 7

Cultivating a Growth Mindset

When you adopt a growth mindset, you accept yourself for who you are while also recognizing that there is always room to build on the qualities that you already possess. A growth mindset is uniquely useful because it is active. Rather than passively accepting yourself for who you are, which would suggest a limiting belief that your traits are set in stone, you bring together self-acceptance and self-improvement. This gives you room to grow without feeling the need to be hard on yourself in the process. You recognize that your long-term goals will take persistent work. This point of view encourages the learning process, which also means embracing mistakes as learning opportunities.

A growth mindset moves you away from feeling the need to be smart just for the sake of being smart to instead focus on self-improvement as the motivating factor. Developing a growth mindset will change your perspective on challenges and mistakes. Instead of viewing these as negatives, they become positives. You will feel encouraged to take on challenges because they are the best opportunities for self-improvement. Mistakes are simply part of the learning process, and they can actually provide unique opportunities for personal growth. Instead of beating yourself up over making mistakes, celebrate mistakes because they are indicators that you are challenging and stretching yourself.

Without a growth mindset, you are more inclined to accept a stagnant life where you believe that things like intelligence and other skills are something that you possess a fixed amount of. This kind of thinking is extremely limiting and can lead to anxiety, depression, and other mental health issues. It also sets you up for failure because when you do not believe that you can change and grow, you are not likely to truly believe that you can achieve your goals, or you may resist setting goals in the first place because nothing seems within reach. This is not a positive state to exist in. If you feel that these sentiments ring true for you, then now is the time to shift your perspective toward cultivating a growth mindset.

Recognizing which type of mindset you currently harbor is the first step in cultivating a growth mindset. Being aware of what a growth mindset looks like and also of your own mindset will allow you to notice when you are limiting yourself because of your way of thinking. When you catch yourself doing this, bring your focus onto the growth mindset model. What is a more positive way to look at this situation that encourages personal growth? The more you are able to consciously shift into this perspective, the more you will begin to live in this mindset.

While it's true that we are all born with certain sets of skills that we are naturally able to do better than other skills, this doesn't mean that we can't learn to improve these other skills that we may not be as naturally gifted in. In fact, hard work and persistence can often sharpen these skills so that they surpass the skill level of someone who is naturally gifted in that area but who does not think that they have to work on developing it.

For example, let's say Stacy is naturally gifted at painting, but Paul is not. Because Stacy lacks a growth mindset, it is her belief that she will always be a better painter than most other people, and because of this, she does not feel motivated to work on improving her craft. Paul, on the other hand, possesses a growth mindset and enjoys painting even though he is not naturally gifted in this area. However, because he has the motivation to improve his painting skills, his hard work pays off, and he eventually becomes a brilliant painter, and his technical skill surpasses Stacy's. It is also Paul's growth mindset that allows him to want to take on challenges head-on instead of shying away from them because of a fear of failure. Paul recognizes that these failures mean that he is putting himself out there, and this encourages him to keep going. He also realizes that he can take these moments of failure and use them to learn and grow in his craft.

Cultivating a growth mindset can be particularly useful for overthinkers because it forces you to embrace challenges and the mistakes you will make along the way. With this shift in perspective toward challenges and mistakes, you will lessen the sense of stress that may be attaching to experimentation and pushing yourself outside of your comfort zone. The more you are able to put yourself out there, the more you will be living in the present moment and, as a result, the less you will overthink.

Acknowledge that challenges will often feel uncomfortable. This is why they are challenging! If you are only doing things that you are already comfortable with, they are not challenging you. The next time you encounter a difficult situation, remembering this will help ease the stress you may be feeling toward it.

The more challenges you are able to work through, the more resilience you will develop. As a result, you will build a strengthened sense of confidence and motivation because there will not be as much fear surrounding the prospects of a challenge. You will also be more willing to do things that you want to do and look inward for guidance as opposed to looking for approval from other people.

Surrounding yourself with a loving support system can also help boost you up after experiencing a setback. Other people can help you look at a situation from a different perspective. Talking through setbacks and struggles you are experiencing with people you trust is often the best way to work through these challenges and learn from them. Just as you provide support to others with your empathy, your support system can do the same for you. You will be able to grow your resilience even more by turning to your support system because they will make it clearer for you to see that you are not alone. Moving forward, you will know that you can lean on others for support, which will make the prospect of failure not as scary.

Self-Compassion

A growth mindset also requires self-compassion. Oftentimes, when we encounter setbacks or make mistakes, we want to just jump straight to self-criticism. But beating yourself up does not encourage growth; rather, it closes you off. We've all heard of tough love, and you might believe that being tough on yourself is the only way that you can push yourself to do better. However, being too tough on yourself actually can have the opposite effect. When you are scolded for something, your brain remembers this and associates negativity with the act. As a result, you become more hesitant to try again.

With a growth mindset, addressing slipups with self-compassion allows for forgiveness. This does not close you off from wanting to try again; rather, it encourages you to take the information you learned from your mistake and keep moving forward.

You may not even realize how often you are being hard on yourself. Often, we get used to being critical of ourselves, which makes it difficult to recognize when we are engaging in these detrimental behaviors. Pay attention to how you react to challenges and setbacks. Are you being kind to yourself, or are you getting frustrated with yourself? For instance, maybe you notice that you tend to give up on challenges quickly. This can be a major red flag that you are being too hard on yourself. When you give up on challenges, you are not letting yourself make mistakes because of the way you beat yourself up after. You may also be giving up on challenges quickly because your negative self-talk is telling you that you will not succeed. These combined factors are results of harsh self-criticism and lead to a fear of trying new things and pushing yourself toward growth.

It's also beneficial to look at how you treat the people you care about when they make mistakes. You will likely find that you treat them with compassion and forgiveness. There is no reason why you can't do the same for yourself. We tend to be our own harshest critics. Because of this, you may have developed some areas of self-loathing. These are the parts of yourself that you wish you could change or always feel frustrated by.

Let's say, for instance, that you cannot stand the way you are constantly apologizing because it makes you feel like you are a pushover. Instead of chastising yourself every time you catch yourself saying "sorry" for every little thing, pause, breathe, and simply acknowledge the behavior. Think about the growth mindset. This is an opportunity to learn. You didn't need to say "sorry" when you passed someone in the doorway. Catching this behavior and gently reminding yourself that this is an area for positive growth will help open you up to modifying this behavior the next time you have the urge to apologize for taking up space.

Limiting Beliefs

Limiting beliefs come from patterns of self-loathing. For instance, let's say because you dislike that you are constantly apologizing, this is an area where you begin to develop self-loathing. Because of this self-loathing, you close yourself off to positive growth and, instead, begin to form negative beliefs about yourself such as *I cannot take up space* or *Nobody cares what I have to say.* These beliefs are not only false, but they prevent you from feeling free to be your authentic self. They also prevent you from taking action, pushing yourself past your comfort zone, and allowing room for personal growth. The first step to counteracting a limiting belief is to ask yourself if the belief is true or not, and from here, you can start to reframe the thought so that it pushes you toward rather than restricts you from the path toward that goal.

The more you live with limiting beliefs, the fewer opportunities you will take and the more negative your state of mind will become. Here's how to shift a limiting belief into a positive belief.

Start by paying attention to any frustrations you have with yourself and any negative beliefs that are attached to these areas of frustration. Focus on one limiting belief at a time, and name that limiting belief. Find a more positive way to look at this assessment. For example, if your limiting belief is "I'm not smart enough to graduate at the top of my class," you can rephrase this in a positive way that supports a growth mindset. Your limiting belief can then turn into a positive one: "I have the power and motivation to work hard and graduate at the top of my class."

This is also a moment where you can turn to your support system. Remember that everyone experiences limiting beliefs from time to time. People often only show the positive sides of their lives to others. As a result, it can seem like everyone else is confident about everything they do and no one else experiences self-doubt. Confiding in someone you trust can not only offer you a fresh perspective and boost in confidence, but it can also show you that there is nothing wrong with you for experiencing moments of self-doubt. It can also allow the other person to share their own limiting beliefs. This way, you can help one another reframe these negative thoughts into positives.

From here, we arrive at tip number nine. **Cultivate a growth mindset and embrace challenges and setbacks to achieve your goals.** In order to move forward, you need to put yourself in challenging situations. Due to the nature of challenging situations, you will, at times, make mistakes, fail, and experience setbacks. However, this is all part of the growth process. When you adopt a growth mindset, you take these obstacles and choose to see the positives in them.

Continuing down this road, you will experience tip number 10. **Keep learning and growing to continue improving your life and achieving your goals.** This is the only way to expand your horizons and open yourself up to new possibilities. Don't limit yourself by staying in your comfort zone—challenge what you think you are capable of, and learn even more about yourself and the world around you!

CHAPTER 8

Developing Self-Discipline

Self-discipline is one of the most crucial skills you need to develop to start reaching your goals. You already know that achieving your goals takes a lot of hard work, and no one can make you work toward them but you. However, it can be difficult to stay on top of this work. Maintaining enough self-discipline to consistently work toward your goals is the hardest part of the process.

A major key to self-discipline lies in thinking through your decisions and then having enough confidence in them to follow through without self-doubt. Because of this, being able to work past overthinking is essential. The more you overthink, the more you will start to second-guess your decisions, and this will get in the way of you following through with them. Thinking about your decisions before you make them will help ensure that you are not making hasty decisions but, rather, well-thought-out ones that you will be more inclined to stick with.

Having a clear goal in mind is a good place to start when making decisions because throughout the process of working toward this goal, you will likely have moments where you feel your self-discipline lacking. Being able to return to your visualized goal will help reset your focus and allow you to persevere through challenges.

Identify your strengths and areas where you can improve. The more honest you are with yourself, the more self-awareness you can have, which is essential when identifying potential areas for improvement. For example, maybe you procrastinate doing paperwork for your job because it is your least favorite part. You lack motivation in this specific area. However, your goal is to get a promotion within the next year, and filling out your paperwork is a necessary step in this process. Visualize getting the promotion you want. This is your long-term goal and something that you can use to help regain your focus. The more clearly you are able to picture yourself reaching your goal, the more motivation you will be able to spark to do the tasks that you would otherwise feel inclined to procrastinate on. Increasing your motivation will increase your self-discipline.

Remove tempting distractions that will get in the way of your self-discipline. If you want to improve your health and fitness, get rid of the junk food in your pantry. If you want to write an article for work by the end of the day, put your phone in the other room and turn off notifications on your laptop. As long as the temptation is there, it will distract you, so set yourself up for success by eliminating it. This will help you stick to the priorities you have set. It becomes so much easier to focus on what you are setting out to do without temptations that you know will get in your way.

Make sure your goals are as specific as possible and have a clear path that you can follow to reach them. This gives you a clear structure to apply your self-discipline to. Taking the time to map out the steps needed to achieve your goal will save you a lot of time (and frustration) in the long run. Going in without a plan, on the other hand, will lead to confusion, frustration, and a lack of motivation, which will get in the way of your ability to practice self-discipline. Break down your goal into smaller tasks that you can feel good about achieving along the way. This gives you tiny wins to celebrate and motivate you to keep going. Having a structured plan gives you something concrete to refocus your attention to when your focus begins to waver. The more achievable each step along the way is, the easier it will be to build up your determination to conquer whichever step you are currently on. When you do not break up a goal into smaller tasks, there may not be any win within reach, and you will not feel motivated to keep working.

Push past excuses by recognizing that they are, in fact, excuses. For example, if you want to take charge of your health, a common excuse is "I don't have time to work out." While you may have a busy schedule, saying that you can't do something is just an excuse. This is an example of a fixed or all-or-nothing mindset, not a growth mindset. Ask yourself how you can make time for a workout. Maybe you need to adjust your workout to be a bit shorter. Maybe you can wake up 30 minutes earlier and use this time to work out. Maybe instead of watching TV after dinner, you can go for a walk. There are many ways that you can make adjustments to accommodate the steps you need to take in order to work toward your goal—it's just a matter of being honest with yourself and having the determination to plan ahead and make it work.

Avoid self-entitlement. People who feel entitled to certain things do not acknowledge that in order to achieve a goal, they actually need to work hard. Putting in the work is a sign of a good growth mindset. When you actively work toward growth, you are recognizing that in order to get what you want in life, you need to (and have the power to) take action. On the other hand, when you feel entitled, you are adopting the belief that you deserve something just because you want it. However, wanting something is just the very first step in achieving it—don't stop here.

Accept that perfection isn't always possible. Actually, most of the time, it is not possible, and this is okay. Even though you have a clear vision of a goal, the end result may not look exactly like what you envisioned. It's best to plan for this so that you don't feel disappointed even after you reach your goal. Opening yourself up to changes along the way to your goal will help you accept change as a whole.

Developing plans for different scenarios that can arise as your journey evolves is a great way to prepare for the changes that may occur along the way. Think about possible scenarios that you may find yourself in. Ask yourself how you want to respond if each of these scenarios happens. Be careful not to overthink this stage in your planning process because these scenarios are still hypothetical at this point. However, the consideration of different scenarios will allow you to feel better prepared and less caught off guard when changes to your plan do occur. This way, your self-discipline will not be thrown off when you hit an unexpected curve.

Remember that failures, mistakes, and unexpected challenges are all part of the process. Allow yourself to work through these experiences without judgment. There are a lot of factors that make up any given outcome; some of these factors will be out of your control. Failure should not stand in your way because it is something normal that everyone experiences from time to time. It is actually an indication that you are challenging yourself to grow. With this in mind, let it inspire you to keep pushing forward. Failure is also not the same thing as defeat. Don't give in to defeat by giving up. Rather, think of this time as a learning opportunity, forgive yourself, and then use what you have learned from your mistakes to keep going with even more confidence.

You can also try working with a coach or a mentor who is trained in the area of teaching self-discipline. Working with someone who has this skill set can offer you a different perspective and valuable guidance. Having another person, whether it be a mentor or friend, can help you stay on track. Oftentimes, when we have another person keeping track of our progress, we tend to stay focused on our goals more. Asking someone you trust to help with this by periodically checking in with you to see where you are in working toward your goal will motivate you to keep going.

Self-discipline is not something that happens overnight. It takes time and practice to get to a place where you feel comfortable and secure with your self-discipline. The best way to build this skill is by practicing it every day. Even practicing it with smaller tasks will help you get more used to it, as long as you are doing it regularly. Self-discipline also requires making certain sacrifices. For instance, if an activity that you regularly engage in is preventing you from maintaining self-discipline, you will need to sacrifice this activity. Setting priorities means being able to let go of the things that are not truly important to you or that do not serve you. This will be challenging, and staying consistent with your self-discipline will be even more challenging. Remember to treat yourself with kindness throughout this process by acknowledging that what you are doing is difficult but also by acknowledging that you have the inner strength to see your goals through.

This will help you develop habits that require a certain level of self-discipline. When forming a habit, it is best to start off slowly. If you aren't used to physical activity, don't try to run 10 miles on your first day at the gym. Gradually progressing toward your goal will help keep you motivated, as each task you accomplish feels achievable for where you are in your process. This also helps you avoid burnout. When you throw yourself too quickly into a new habit, you will burn out quicker. It will seem impossible to maintain, so you will feel more inclined to give up. Set yourself up for success by developing new habits gradually.

Self-discipline encourages delayed gratification, which can be a challenging prospect for some people. With delayed gratification, you put off short-term rewards in favor of more meaningful long-term rewards. For example, maybe your long-term goal is to quit smoking. You know that once you successfully quit, you will feel so much better, but you are craving a cigarette right now. You can either give in to temptation and have the cigarette now, or you can push past this temptation using self-discipline in favor of reaching your long-term goal more quickly.

Visualizing your long-term goal in these moments can help you stick with your plan and maintain your self-discipline. The more within reach and specific your visualization feels, the easier it will be to recognize the benefits of delayed gratification. For me, a major temptation is sweets. While I enjoy sweets while I'm eating them, they always make me feel bad about 30 minutes afterward. Because I have this self-awareness, I think about how I will eventually feel if I eat sweet junk food versus if I opt for a healthy snack. Since I am able to clearly imagine both scenarios and recognize which decision is the obvious one for delayed gratification, it is easier for me to make the right decision to stick to my long-term goal of making healthy choices.

Overcoming Procrastination

Developing Habits and Routines

Developing habits and routines is an important step in managing your goals and practicing regular self-discipline. The stronger your habits and routines, the easier they become to maintain. However, getting to this point takes time and effort. Contrary to popular belief, there is no fixed time to develop a habit. In reality, developing a habit will take different amounts of time depending on the individual and the habit itself. It's important not to beat yourself up over slipups. This is normal, and everyone has their own experience of ups and downs when trying to develop a habit. Forgiving yourself is the best way to move forward with your goal, because the more frustrated you get with yourself over mistakes, the more shame and stress you will begin to associate with the habit, which will leave you more hesitant to keep it up.

Since self-discipline can help you develop habits that move you toward your long-term goals, it can play a significant role in your ability to follow your dreams and become the person you want to be. Once you integrate your new habits into your daily life, you are making changes to your lifestyle that support your values and purpose.

Working on developing habits can provide many benefits for you in addition to helping you work toward your goals, such as improving your mental health. The more structure you are able to maintain in your daily schedule, the more balanced, steady, and in control of your own life you will begin to feel. For instance, maintaining a regular bedtime can be hugely beneficial to both your mental and physical health, as this allows your body to get used to when it is time to go to sleep. On the other hand, if you go to sleep at different times every night, your body does not develop a natural circadian rhythm, and as a result, it is harder for your body to get a restful night's sleep. Not getting sufficient sleep can then lead to a myriad of mental and physical health issues.

It can be helpful to organize your routines into two categories: primary and secondary. Your primary routines are your habits that are of utmost importance to you to maintain. Some examples of primary routines include

- bedtime
- healthy diet
- regular exercise
- meditation

Primary routines will look different for everyone depending on what each individual's priorities are. The same holds true for secondary routines. Secondary routines are your habits that are important to you but that you are willing to compromise every now and then if need be. Some examples of secondary routines include

- reading
- cooking
- cleaning
- studying

When you maintain a regular routine, you can actually fit more into your day because routines tend to boost confidence, which boosts motivation and productivity. You may find, for example, that when you fall into a routine of exercising every morning, you are able to get more work done afterward. It can be tempting to stray from your primary routines, such as exercising every morning, in order to get something else done, such as a work project.

However, you likely do have time for both activities. Choosing to keep up with your exercise routine can then boost your productivity so that when you do get to your work, you are able to finish it quicker. On the other hand, if you jump straight into your work, you may feel distracted or unmotivated because you are missing your daily exercise routine.

Habits are also best formed when you are able to do your chosen activity at the same time every day. For instance, exercising every morning will be easier for you to maintain than simply saying you want to exercise every day but not having a dedicated time set aside for this activity. Not having a regular schedule for a habit that you want to form will leave you debating throughout the day when you should do the activity. Sticking to a schedule eliminates the time wasted overthinking this decision.

Establishing daily routines ensures that you are maintaining your priorities. Without daily routines, it's easier to unintentionally prioritize less meaningful tasks and disregard the tasks that are more important to you. Routines can help you live more authentically because you are regularly addressing your priorities. Pay attention to your routines. Even if you have not intentionally set your routines yet, you likely have some sort of daily routine, whether it be waking up and walking the dog or watching TV during dinner. Write down all the routines you notice. Then go through your list and think about how important each routine is for you. How are these routines serving you? You may find that some of your routines are not serving you in any way at all. In fact, certain routines may be taking away from your real priorities. From here, you can begin to go through what you would like your primary and secondary routines to look like. Once you have established these and have gotten rid of the routines that are not serving you, you can organize your priorities and come up with a schedule.

Remember that when first making a schedule, it is likely going to evolve. Allow yourself some wiggle room for change in your schedule as you figure out how everything is going to work. You often need to actually go through your day according to your schedule in order to understand how that proposed schedule would work. Be patient with yourself but persistent. If something is important to you, trust that you will find a way to fit it into your daily schedule, but don't get frustrated with yourself if figuring out a time when you can address this priority takes a little while.

Creating an environment that sets you up for success is well worth the time. If you are in the right mindset, feeling motivated, and you have a plan but your physical environment is disorganized and full of distractions, all your hard work can seem to go out the window. Set up an environment that reflects your determined mindset. This will reinforce it rather than clash with it. Build your environment around the task at hand. You can do this by eliminating distractions and clutter so that your attention is not split between your goal and everything that's happening in your physical environment. The more distractions present, the more you have to take in, and the less you can focus on what you are trying to stay focused on.

When you feel distracted while trying to develop a habit, take a moment to bring your attention to mindfulness. This will help get you centered back to the present and to the task at hand. Allow whatever distraction is on your mind to simply pass along, free from judgment. Once it has moved on, use something sensorial to bring you back to the present. What can you notice about your present environment? Any smells, sounds, or textures that stand out to you? Allow yourself to focus on these observations for a few moments. This will ensure that your mind is fully present. From here, refocusing on your task will be much easier.

Developing habits and routines can actually improve your physical health. In a 2014 study conducted by Virginia Adams O'Connell, a sample of college students "who engaged in 'healthy' daily routines like regular exercise and getting an average of seven hours of sleep per night were less likely to get sick during the study than students who did not" (Reisenwitzn.d.). Other studies have similarly tracked the correlation between routine and illness and found that people who maintain healthy routines tend to encounter fewer illnesses (Reisenwitzn.d.). Make sure that your habits are supporting a healthy lifestyle and alter them if they are not.

Developing habits and routines at a young age is extremely beneficial for children and can help them get used to developing and maintaining healthy habits into adulthood. Children are like sponges—they soak up so much information and knowledge so readily. For instance, kids who grow up in a bilingual household are quickly able to learn two languages at once, whereas learning a new language becomes more of a challenge the older we get. The same idea applies to habit-building practices. Children who grow up with a certain level of structure are able to readily build their self-discipline. Assuming they maintain these types of habits, they are more used to and willing to apply self-discipline to their work as adults because they are already so familiar with the tools needed to develop self-discipline and stick to routines that support their goals. The more healthy habits and routines a child has, the more they will benefit from outcomes like a healthy sleep routine, healthy eating habits, and self-discipline with schoolwork because they are used to a balanced lifestyle.

Habits are a significant stress management tool. When you have routines and habits, you feel more prepared because you have more structure and more of a solid plan. As a result, you tend to feel less stressed. The more stressed you feel on a daily basis, the more you risk a negative impact on your health. For instance, according to health writer Michelle Pugle, chronic stress is associated with high blood pressure. Over time, if high blood pressure is not treated, you increase your risk of developing more severe medical conditions like heart disease (Pugle 2021). Eliminating as much chronic stress as possible reduces these types of medical risks, as well as improves your mood, overall mental health, and general well-being.

Without stress getting in the way of your health, factors like cognitive function, energy levels, and immunity improve. Routines positively impact factors like sleep and diet as well, which contribute to your general health and well-being. For example, according to Northwestern Medicine (2022), when you maintain a routine, you are more likely to have a more regular sleep schedule, which tends to result in improved quality and quantity of sleep. Healthy sleep habits promote many different physical and mental health benefits.

Routines can also help promote healthy eating. When you don't have a routine and have less of a plan, you are more likely to opt for easy but unhealthy food choices like a bag of chips instead of a nutritious meal or snack that you would get by planning ahead. Developing healthy grocery shopping habits can help you move toward making healthier choices because you are able to go into the store with a plan. In doing so, you are more prepared to resist the temptation to purchase unhealthy food at the store. As a result, you will eliminate unhealthy temptations from your home altogether.

You're also more prepared to get regular exercise when you have a routine because you have worked out how you will fit this into your schedule. If you tell yourself you want to start exercising, but do not have a game plan regarding how you are going to develop this habit as part of your daily routine, it is much harder to stick with it, and you will waste time trying to figure out on the fly when to go to the gym. On the other hand, if you commit to working out every day at 10 a.m., for instance, you will have a more solid game plan and it will be easier to commit to this goal every day. Since you have already sorted out this time in your schedule, you can work around this activity. This is especially beneficial if exercise is a priority for you. Developing routines for your priorities will help keep you focused on the things that matter the most to you, and from here, you can schedule time for other activities that are not as high on your priority list.

Tip number 11 is all about your motivation and perseverance to keep working toward your goals. **Build self-discipline and willpower to stay focused and overcome procrastination.** The more you are able to work on building your self-discipline, the more you will be able to do, which will then open you up for more experiences and more challenges.

CHAPTER 9

Improving Sleep Habits

Sleep can be a major source of discomfort for overthinkers. Sources of overthinking can easily pop up in your mind as you lay in bed at night. The more you overthink, the more stressed you will feel, making it nearly impossible to fall asleep. On top of this, the more time it takes you to fall asleep, the more you may begin to feel anxiety surrounding the fact that you are not yet asleep. Once these fears begin to creep in, you can start to overthink about how you might feel in the morning after not having gotten a good night's rest. The more you begin to overthink, the harder it becomes to stop overthinking. This sets you up for an unsatisfactory night's sleep.

So how do you avoid this detrimental cycle? Luckily, there are many different techniques that are geared toward exactly this.

One such technique involves choosing a word to repeat whenever your mind begins to wander to intrusive thoughts. Your chosen word can be almost anything as long as it is not tied to an emotion for you. For example, articles can be useful, such as "an" or "the" because they do not have connotations with emotions. You can even use a made-up word or nonsensical sound, like "scah" or "vee." When you start to experience an intrusive thought, repeat your word so that it blocks out any other thoughts. Sometimes repeating your word more quickly can help with this. Experiment with tempo, and find what works best for you.

You can also visualize a shape to associate with your word. Let's say your word is "scah" and your shape is a circle. Every time you repeat your word, visualize a circle. The addition of the visualization will help block out images that your intrusive thoughts may bring into your mind.

You can also use visualization as a different technique in which you imagine a peaceful scene. With this visualization, you will want to be as specific as possible and use all of your senses to create the scene. For example, if you choose a beach scene, you will want to visualize the color and texture of the sand, how it feels when you run your hand through it, how the ocean breeze smells, how the wind feels as it breezes through your hair, the different sizes of seashells buried around you in the sand, and the sound of the waves gently crashing onto the shore. The more sensory details you are able to create, the harder it will become for intrusive thoughts to interfere with your immersion in your peaceful place.

Be consistent with your sleep routine. Aim to get about seven to eight hours of sleep per night. Setting a bedtime and also a time to wake up will help get your body into a routine. Once your body gets used to this routine, your circadian rhythm—your body's internal clock that naturally makes you sleepy at a certain time and more alert at a certain time—will regulate according to your determined schedule. This will make sleep come much easier and also improve the quality of sleep you're getting. As a result, you will feel more well-rested, focused, and present throughout your day. However, your circadian rhythm cannot maintain this balance if you do not adhere to the schedule you have set.

Pay attention to when you naturally become tired. Try going to sleep at this time. If you try to go to sleep when you are not yet tired, you are more likely to have to deal with things like overthinking at bedtime and frustration from not being able to fall asleep. If this happens, get up, do a relaxing activity that does not involve a screen, such as listening to relaxing music or reading. Once you begin to feel tired, try going back to sleep.

When establishing your sleep schedule, you may also want to set an alarm for when you want to wake up. Setting an alarm will ensure that you are waking up at a consistent time, which will help your body become accustomed to your sleep routine. Once your body falls comfortably into this routine, you may notice that you are waking up at your designated wake-up time even without an alarm.

Pay attention to the food and drinks you are consuming and what time you are consuming them. Eating a heavy meal or drinking alcohol right before bed often disrupts sleep. Likewise, do not try to go to bed when you are hungry. The more comfortable you feel at bedtime, the more of a relaxed state your body is able to sink into, and the more restful a night's sleep you will be able to achieve.

Caffeine and nicotine will also cause disruptive sleep, as these are stimulants and will keep your body alert instead of relaxed. While alcohol is not a stimulant and may make you feel sleepy, it actually does not help with sleep. You may notice that when you consume alcohol before bed, you fall asleep faster, but you do not feel rested in the morning. This is because alcohol tends to cause disruptive sleep throughout the night after you have initially fallen asleep.

Create the best environment for sleep. Consider all the environmental factors that may be getting in the way of your sleep. For instance, if a lot of light comes in through your shades, consider switching them out for blackout curtains. Your circadian rhythm is closely tied to lightness and darkness, so the more you can regulate the light that comes into your bedroom, the more control you can have over regulating your circadian rhythm. This also goes for screen time. The more light from a screen you are exposed to closer to bedtime, the more disrupted your circadian rhythm will be. If there are sources of light within your bedroom, such as a clock, make sure to cover these as well. Although it may not seem like hardly any light at all, these sources of light can actually have a significant effect on your circadian rhythm and ability to fall asleep.

Having a fan or noise machine that plays soft, soothing sounds can be particularly helpful for overthinkers because it gives you something concrete to focus on when negative self-talk begins to creep in. You may instead want to try sleeping with earplugs, especially if there tends to be a lot of noise when you are trying to fall asleep. You can purchase wax or wax-cotton blended earplugs that mold to your ears. You may prefer these types of earplugs over regular foam earplugs because they tend to stay put in your ears more, even if you toss and turn in your sleep. Make sure to turn off or silence your cell phone before bed so that you are not receiving notifications that can disrupt your sleep.

Keep your bedroom at a comfortable temperature. I like to keep my room a little cooler than usual at night so that I don't become hot under the blankets. The more comfortable a temperature you are able to maintain in your bedroom, the less disruptive changes in temperature will be for your sleep.

When you do not yet have a balanced sleep schedule, you may feel tired during the day. Napping can seem like a good way to overcome daytime sleepiness; however, the more you nap during the day, the harder it will be to maintain a regular sleep schedule and get a good night's rest. Try to avoid napping as much as possible, and if you do need to nap, set an alarm to ensure that your nap does not exceed one hour. Avoid naps altogether in the late afternoon or evening.

Maintaining a regular exercise routine can help you get a more restful night's sleep. This can be as simple as going for a 20-minute walk. However, it is best to get your physical activity in earlier in the day so that you are not exercising before bed, which can actually get in the way of falling asleep because you are going to bed in a heightened state of stimulation. The more regular your exercise routine is, the more you will be able to maintain it as a habit, and the more your body will feel accustomed to incorporating this into your circadian rhythm.

If you have nagging thoughts that you cannot seem to redirect, try writing them down in a journal before you go to bed. This way, you can tell yourself that you will address these worries tomorrow and be able to move forward, focusing on getting a good night's sleep. The more stress management you are able to incorporate into your daily life, the less worry you will experience at bedtime, and the easier sleep will come. Meditation before bed can help tremendously in easing your mind and getting yourself into a relaxed state for bedtime. You can incorporate meditation into your daily bedtime routine. This way, you can work toward forming a habit by having a set time to practice meditation every day as well as use meditation to benefit your sleep. This can take as little as five to ten minutes—the most important thing is the maintenance of the practice.

Diet and Sleep

Your diet actually plays a larger role in your sleep health than you might imagine. When you maintain a balanced diet, you are giving your body the vitamins and nutrients it needs to function properly. On the other hand, if you do not consume a balanced diet, your body may be lacking in some nutrients that could help you get a better night's rest. Some nutrients and supplements that promote healthy sleep include the following:

- tryptophan
- magnesium
- melatonin
- L-theanine
- valerian root
- ashwagandha
- ginkgo biloba
- herbs such as chamomile and passionflower
- lavender for its soothing scent

Getting a balanced diet is all about variety. Eating different types of whole foods, such as lean proteins, healthy fats, vegetables, fruits, and whole grains, will ensure that you are providing your body everything it needs to function at its highest level—and this includes its ability to get good sleep, both in quantity and quality.

There are also certain foods that you may want to avoid before bedtime, as they can be disruptive for some people. Some examples of these foods include

- high-fat foods
- heavy foods
- spicy foods
- sugar
- caffeine
- alcohol

These foods tend to be more difficult to digest, which can lead to discomfort. Eating foods that are easier to digest at dinner will help ensure that your body is in its most relaxed state when it's time for bed.

If you are someone who is overweight, you are at a higher risk of developing sleep apnea, which is a sleep disorder that involves irregular breathing patterns. People with sleep apnea experience breathing that stops and starts rather than flowing regularly. This causes disruptions in sleep, leaving you feeling tired during the day. An indicator that you may have sleep apnea is heavy snoring. Maintaining a balanced diet and regular exercise will help keep your body healthy and reduce the risk or symptoms of sleep apnea.

Tip number 12 is to **develop healthy sleep habits to improve sleep quality and quantity.** When you are well-rested, you are able to be more alert and productive and to live more as your authentic self because you feel happier and healthier. Sleep affects so many different aspects of our lives that we often don't consider, so getting proper sleep will significantly improve your overall well-being. The key is in consistency. Stick with a schedule and routine for your sleep patterns, and you will feel the difference—your motivation will be the most crucial factor in your ability to maintain healthy sleep habits.

CHAPTER 10

Boosting Productivity and Creativity

As you know by now, overthinking can be a difficult cycle to break, and breaking free from this habit is something that takes time and effort. A major reason why overthinking occurs is because of the need to achieve perfection. When you fear making mistakes, you overthink all the ways that something can go wrong. When you do make a mistake, you overthink it by getting stuck in the frustration surrounding the mistake instead of forgiving yourself and moving forward. The more frustrated you get with yourself over mistakes, the more anxiety you begin to associate with mistakes. This anxiety can get in the way of you trying things outside of your comfort zone because you are familiar with the unpleasant feeling of frustration you know you'll get if you make a mistake. As a result, you get less done. This is why productivity is so severely thwarted by overthinking.

The more you overthink, the more used to this behavior you become. As a result, things that hold little-to-no significance will start to get in your way. For instance, something as simple and insignificant as placing an order at the checkout can become a point of anxiety. Overthinking takes your attention away from the decisions that matter and your ability to act on those decisions.

Pay attention to how much time you spend thinking about doing something versus how much time you actually spend doing it. While it's beneficial to plan ahead and come up with a road map for certain tasks, you don't want to cross over into overthinking. If you find that you are not actually getting a lot done, it may be because overthinking is getting in the way of you taking action and being productive.

Also pay attention to what tasks you are spending significant amounts of time thinking through. You may find that you are overthinking things that simply do not matter. For example, you may spend a lot of time stressing out about what to caption a social media post. Taking the time to assess what you are spending your focus on can help you recognize where you need to let go. The more insignificant scenarios you can allow yourself to stop overthinking and move forward with a simple decision, the more time and energy you will have to focus on what matters most to you.

Overthinking is a way to protect you from making mistakes. The key to overcoming overthinking is to change your outlook on mistakes. When you are able to view mistakes as part of the learning process, you will be less inclined to overthink because you are reducing the fear that surrounds challenges and the unknown.

Tapping into your creative side can actually help boost your productivity and get you out of an overthinking cycle. There are ways to help spark your creativity that you can apply to your productivity and problem-solving.

Oftentimes, when you apply direct pressure to a problem, you aren't able to find a solution. Instead, allowing some distance between yourself and the problem lets you see a different perspective. If you are struggling with something that you need to figure out, take a break and focus on something else. This break will allow your mind to reset, and in doing so, it opens up to a wider variety of potential solutions. For instance, if you are trying to find a solution for a problem at work and cannot seem to figure out what to do, give yourself a break to just relax. When you are in a more relaxed state, without the problem occupying the majority of your mental capacity, a creative solution that you had not previously considered may come to you more seamlessly. Distancing yourself temporarily from a problem can give you the mental clarity you need for your creativity to come through.

A little space to be creative

You are more creative during your peak hours. This is another reason why you should choose to tackle your most important and urgent tasks during the time of day you feel most productive—this is the time when you are also your most creative! The combination of creativity and productivity will allow you to accomplish more, both in quantity and quality.

Placing certain constraints on yourself can actually help enhance your creative side. Although it may seem like working with zero rules or regulations in place would promote the highest levels of creativity, this is actually not typically the case. When you have some limitations, whether it be materials to work with or a time frame, you are forced to get creative.

For example, if you asked a chef to cook a meal using any ingredients he wanted, with no time constraints, and in a kitchen of his choice, he would likely opt for a meal that is both gourmet and that he feels comfortable with. On the other hand, if you asked that same chef to cook a meal using a limited number of ingredients that he did not have a say in choosing, in one hour, and in a nonprofessional kitchen, he would simply have to get creative. These kinds of situations where certain limitations are put on you can bring out a result that you wouldn't have otherwise thought to produce.

Without any kind of constraints, your creativity isn't as necessary to your situation. However, it's all about finding the right balance. You don't want to limit yourself too much, or your creativity will be limited. But finding that happy medium can skyrocket your creative potential and boost your productivity in the process.

Creativity requires that you are in a certain state of mind. You cannot unleash your creative potential if you are under too much stress. Getting yourself into a state of mind so that your brain produces serotonin and dopamine puts you in a more relaxed state that is conducive to creativity. When you feel stressed, you tend to gravitate toward things you are comfortable with; however, it is when you push yourself past these comfort boundaries that you really begin to utilize your creative prowess. According to journalist Karla Lant (2018), having healthy amounts of serotonin and dopamine usually results in elevated mood and self-confidence, a relaxed energy, and a sense of heightened inspiration.

When you are in a creative mindset, you are able to make connections you would not otherwise make because you are open to new perspectives. These connections and shifts in perspective that you experience when in a creative state provide an element of the unexpected in your work—this is what makes the work creative. You are not making the obvious choices. Try writing these unexpected connections down in a mind map. To make your mind map, write down your initial ideas. Then, create a branch to other ideas that come from these ideas. This way, you will be able to more easily visualize your creative process.

The Role of Organization

Setting goals and managing your time play significant roles in your productivity. They can help you focus on honing important skills that are needed to become your most productive and creative self.

Make a goal to get organized. Being specific about the ways in which you intend to get organized is important so that you have a clear goal and plan that you can stick to. For example, writing out a daily priorities list can be a useful organizational tool for you, so your goal might be, "Every evening, I will write out my daily priorities list for the following day." It can be beneficial to work on your organizational goal at the same time every day so that it more seamlessly becomes a habit.

Organize your priorities according to importance level and also urgency level. As discussed in Chapter 5, determining importance and urgency levels for your daily tasks will help keep you focused on your real priorities instead of spending too much time on tasks that ultimately do not hold much significance. This will allow you to understand your priorities, which is an important first step you need to take before you can start working toward your various goals. A priority goal can be something like, "I will complete my important and urgent tasks, allowing myself breaks if needed, before moving onto tasks that are lower on my priority list."

Setting goals aimed at overcoming distractions can also help boost your productivity. Once you organize a list of priorities, it is important that you focus your attention on these tasks, one at a time, without letting distractions get in the way. Pay attention to what types of distractions tend to get in the way of your progress the most. For example, maybe when you're trying to work and your phone is on your desk constantly sending you notifications, it's difficult to focus on the task at hand because the temptation of checking those notifications is too strong. This is totally normal and not something you should get frustrated with yourself for.

Instead, set a distraction goal that eliminates the problem. For this situation, you might want to make an organizational goal to only allow your work at your workspace. If you work at a desk, this means your cell phone cannot be on the desk. While you're working, turn off notifications on your phone (or turn off your phone) so that you do not hear the notifications going off at all. Your desk and the time you have allotted to focusing on your work becomes organized and primed for optimal results when you eliminate distractors. The more committed to this goal you are, the more seamlessly the habit will form.

Setting goals regarding planning will help with your time management and help you feel prepared—even when unexpected challenges arise. Making planning goals for complex tasks can be particularly useful. For example, if you have a work project that you know you will be working on over the span of a month, you will need to establish certain deadlines for yourself. A specific planning goal for this complex project can look like, "I will check in with my department at the end of every week." This planning strategy ensures that everyone working on the project is on the same page throughout the process, which will also help eliminate possible setbacks. Planning ahead is the first step in getting ahead of a complex task. Making sure to maintain planning goals is the best way to ensure that you are staying ahead and following through with your initial planning strategies.

These organizational strategies will help you take control over your time management and finish tasks that are priorities for you. The more organizational tools like these you utilize, the more confident you will feel, and the more quickly and easily you will accomplish your tasks. You will also feel better prepared for whatever may come your way, get more tasks done, eliminate distractions that do not serve you, and get the most out of any given situation.

It's also essential to schedule regular breaks and downtime. This time will help keep you functioning at your most productive level by creating balance. In order to maintain productivity, you need mental breaks. When you relax and think about things other than what you are currently working on, your brain is able to recharge. However, remember that this is only applicable if you are setting time limits for your breaks; taking a scheduled break is not the same thing as getting distracted by your phone or the TV periodically while you're working. When you return to your work after taking a scheduled break, you will find that you feel more productive and more creative after having some intentional time away from your work.

This brings us to the 13th and final tip. **Take breaks and incorporate downtime to recharge and boost productivity and creativity.** While it may initially seem counterintuitive, allowing yourself time to rest and reset is actually an essential part of maintaining focus for longer stretches of time. It will not only improve the quantity of your work but also the quality of it, as breaking from your work activates your creative side and brings something new to the table.

Conclusion

We all get stuck in detrimental thought patterns from time to time. However, it is your ability to reframe these thoughts into positives that will set you apart and allow you to move forward without letting them consume you. The more you are able to practice challenging overthinking, the more you will be able to stick to your goals and create the life you want (and deserve) to be living. You now have all the tools to set yourself up for success and get away from overthinking habits. Take pride in your determination to grow and all that you have managed to accomplish. Remember that overcoming overthinking isn't easy! Thoughts hold a great deal of power—the key is to reframe your thoughts to let this power serve you. When in doubt, remember the 13 tips.

1. Cultivate gratitude to focus on the positive and create a more positive mindset.
2. Practice self-compassion and forgive yourself for mistakes and failures.
3. Practice mindfulness daily to quiet the mind and increase self-awareness.

4. Identify and challenge negative thought patterns and self-talk to reframe your thinking.
5. Embrace imperfection and let go of the need for control to overcome perfectionism.
6. Prioritize tasks and manage your time effectively to reduce stress and increase productivity.
7. Align your goals and actions with your values and purpose to find meaning and fulfillment.
8. Develop strong communication skills to build better relationships and manage conflict.
9. Cultivate a growth mindset and embrace challenges and setbacks to achieve your goals.
10. Keep learning and growing to continue improving your life and achieving your goals.
11. Build self-discipline and willpower to stay focused and overcome procrastination.
12. Develop healthy sleep habits to improve sleep quality and quantity.
13. Take breaks and incorporate downtime to recharge and boost productivity and creativity.

Challenging negative thought patterns and cultivating positivity will help you work toward building the life you truly want to live. Taking charge of your thoughts will help clear your mind to focus on what you want to achieve and how you want to go about reaching these goals. Negative thoughts only have power if you give them power. When you choose to give attention instead to positivity, it will reflect in your mindset and your actions.

Choosing to do things you're proud of improves your mood, drive, and overall sense of well-being. Finding ways to incorporate positivity in your everyday life makes you feel more positive. In a similar sense, the more positivity you put out into the world, the more positivity you receive in return. You will see that the more you are able to practice positivity, the stronger this cycle will grow; the more positive actions you perform, the better you will feel, and, as a result, the more positive actions you will feel inspired to do.

Of course, the same holds true with negativity. If you send out negativity, the worse you will feel, and then the more your actions will be driven by negativity. However, if you find yourself in this cycle, make the conscious decision to do something that inspires positivity. This immediately shifts the cycle and grounds you in positive energy. Take the time to check in with yourself, whether it be through meditation, cultivating your creativity, or spending time doing another positive activity you enjoy. Remember that you can always take action to start feeling like your true, positive self once again—all you need to do is take the time to focus on the good.

When you feel good about yourself and how you make decisions, you will get more used to living life on your own terms. This means doing the things that make you feel happy—whatever these things may be. Positivity will then become second-nature for you, inspiring you to live your life based on your positive values.

Loving yourself is the first step. When you fully accept yourself, you are more readily able to check in on yourself. When you regularly check in with your own well-being, you are able to maintain reduced stress, increased happiness, and also improved productivity. This is because in order to perform at your highest level, you need to feel your best. Trying to push yourself further and further without taking time to check in with yourself and pay attention to your needs will not get you to where you want to be. Although it may initially seem counterintuitive, taking the time to practice self-care actually boosts your productivity. Being able to maintain a healthy balance of inward and outward focus will set you on the path to discover your full potential, while also living a happy and fulfilled life.

Maintaining this balance will allow you to also increase productivity and happiness while reducing stress by making you feel more comfortable pushing yourself outside of your comfort zone. When you spend all your time doing things you already know how to do, you are limiting your growth. On the other hand, when you step outside of your typical boundaries, you are encouraging yourself to learn by experiencing something new. For example, let's say you go from point A to point B every day. You know exactly what to expect, and so you move through these motions on autopilot. However, let's say one day you decide to instead go from point A to point C before arriving at point B. This change expands your horizons and experiences, and it is the only way to grow.

The same idea applies to creativity and productivity, because when you alter the way you look at something, you begin to approach it with a different perspective instead of the most obvious perspective. This is the heart of creativity, and it can often provide the most valuable solutions. Apply this principle to problem-solving when you are feeling stuck. Mentally, this nonlinear perspective change applies when you take a break from what you are working on. When you come back to your work, your perspective is fresh and opened up to new possibilities and pathways.

Don't limit yourself by staying in your comfort zone. Achieving your goals will require you to take this leap that will provide you new perspectives and experiences. When you are able to push through a challenge, the results are so rewarding, but taking that first step can be scary. When you feel yourself hesitating to take this step, remind yourself of a time when you pushed past your comfort zone in order to achieve a goal. How did it feel when you reached that goal?

Typically, the idea of stepping outside of your comfort zone is scarier than the actual act of doing so, because there is a mental block telling you that you can't do something outside of your comfort zone. However, in reality, once you actually do push yourself out of your comfort zone, you realize that you can, in fact, do the thing that you were nervous to do, because you are actually doing it. Overcoming these obstacles releases you from the fear of failure. The more you practice taking steps outside of your comfort zone and the more you tell yourself that you are capable of overcoming challenges, the more your confidence will grow. As a result, the more you will be willing to try new things, and the more actively you will pursue your goals.

You can use affirmations to help guide yourself toward specific goals. For instance, if you are feeling a little out-of-touch with yourself and want to practice checking in on yourself more regularly, there are certain affirmations that can help remind you to do so. Here are some examples of how affirmations can help guide you in any occasion.

To increase self-awareness or check in with yourself:

- I pay attention to what I need.
- I can take things at my own pace.
- I work toward understanding myself better.
- I accept my thoughts and feelings.
- My mind and body are in harmony.
- I give power to positive thinking.
- I am aware of the journey I am on.
- I can learn from self-reflection.
- I accept responsibility for my intentional actions.
- I am in charge of my life.

To feel physically well:

- I feel positive energy radiate through my body.
- Every breath rejuvenates me.
- My body is strong and resilient.
- I nourish my body with the fuel it needs.
- I treat my body with kindness.

- I listen to and am in harmony with what my body tells me.
- My body and mind are connected.

To motivate you toward your goals:

- I work for my successes.
- I push forward, no matter the outcome or obstacles.
- I am on the right path.
- I can achieve what I set my mind to.
- I am not limited by my thoughts.
- My creativity shines.
- I always put forward my best effort.
- I have all the tools to keep learning and growing.

To practice self-love:

- I am worthy of great things.
- I love every aspect of myself.
- I am confident and capable.
- I forgive myself.
- I learn from my mistakes.
- I do not need to change myself for anyone.
- I am valuable and valued just as I am.
- I am beautiful inside and out.
- I am in control of my own thoughts.

To cultivate gratitude for those around you:

- I forgive others.

- I surround myself with positive people.
- I have so much to learn from others.
- I have a strong support system.
- I am interested in what others have to say.
- I deserve the positive relationships in my life.
- I accept my loved ones for who they are.
- I love all the aspects of my partner that make them unique.
- I don't want or need to change anyone.

What you tell yourself strengthens your belief systems, which then affects your actions. The more you practice positivity through affirmations, the more you will begin to believe these positive ideas, which will then allow you to take action to make them true. For example, the more you tell yourself "I surround myself with positive people," the more you believe it, and then the more you actually take steps to do so. It works by increasing your awareness surrounding this specific goal and making you feel confident in your ability to achieve this goal. When you believe that you can achieve your goals, you will take the steps needed to work toward your goals. Reinforcing your positive beliefs is the first step in taking actions to achieve your goals. Remember that you must first believe you are capable of reaching your goals in order to actually achieve them.

Making your own affirmations can also be a helpful process because it makes you identify a specific area that you would like to work on and then come up with an affirmation that is tailored toward your needs in that area. For instance, maybe you find that you often beat yourself up over small mistakes. This is an area where you can improve on treating yourself with kindness. It is also an area where you can improve on shifting into more of a growth mindset.

Once you identify the area for improvement, try to think of a positive way of looking at it. Instead of saying "I always make mistakes," you could say "I learn from my mistakes." This way, you are shifting the way you view mistakes to the positive.

Write down your affirmations. It can help to have an affirmation journal so that you have one place specifically dedicated to affirmations. Once you have gathered some affirmations and have practiced writing down your own affirmations, you can always return to them when needed.

Remember to always write your affirmations in the present tense. Even if your affirmation is more of a goal that you want to work toward, phrasing it in the present puts you in that place. If you want to learn from your mistakes but do not feel like you currently do so, phrasing your affirmations in the present can help you actually believe that you can do so, and that you can start doing so now. On the other hand, phrasing an affirmation in the future tense is not as useful because it gives you an excuse to put off your goal. Saying "I will start to learn from my mistakes" may put you in a mindset that this is a future goal that will eventually come to fruition; however, you are only able to bring about this positive change when you actually take action to learn from your mistakes, not just think about doing it in the future.

Refrain from beginning affirmations with "I need." Affirmations are meant to affirm; therefore, you should try to phrase them as if you are already doing what it is you want to be doing. Because they are affirming statements, they are also meant to express a certain amount of gratitude. You already have all the tools you need to achieve your goal. Sometimes saying "I need" adds a level of desperation or longing that doesn't need to be there and that can actually get in the way of your sense of peace with the goal in mind.

Keep your affirmations simple. The easier they are to remember and make sense of, the more often you will be able to repeat them to yourself throughout your day as needed. Affirmations are meant to be easily accessed. If you have a goal that is multifaceted and want to use affirmations to help motivate you toward this goal, it is often best to split up the different facets of your goal into separate affirmations. For example, let's say a major goal of yours is active self-acceptance. A couple of pathways you have identified to work toward your goal are to express your thoughts and opinions more openly and to accept your emotions as valid instead of pushing them away. Although these two thoughts are related, you will want to break them up into more bite-sized pieces when phrasing them as affirmations. These affirmations could look like "I speak up for myself" and "My emotions are valid."

Be patient. It can take time for your affirmations to have their intended effect. Changing behaviors or thought patterns doesn't happen overnight. Set yourself up for success by making your affirmations manageable and realistic. If your affirmation is too far removed from what you are realistically able to believe, it is less likely to do anything for you. In this case, you can find ways to break down the goal into progressive affirmations. This way, you can progressively build your confidence instead of trying to force yourself to believe something that you realistically do not yet.

Behavior change is all about the art of becoming more intentional. Setting goals and doing things to work toward these goals, like creating affirmations, gets you out of autopilot and into a more intentional headspace. Oftentimes, it is easy to get stuck on autopilot. While developing certain habits can be positive for your life and something you may want to work toward building, sometimes habits can also get you into this type of autopilot mode. This happens when you simply move through the motions of something you are already very accustomed to, instead of remaining present in the moment. For instance, if you take the subway to work every day, you likely take the exact same route every morning, and doing so allows you to move through the motions on autopilot in order to eventually arrive at work. You are not making any observations on the world around you or remaining open to the present moment. This type of automatic routine pulls you away from intentional living and puts you in the passenger seat of your own life.

Acting intentionally means you get to live your life according to your own priorities, which puts you completely in charge of your life choices. Doing so ultimately allows you to ask yourself what you want out of life and then do what you need in order to get to this place.

In order to change your behaviors, you will need to first identify your current behaviors. Doing so keeps you self-aware and lets you identify areas where you would like to see some improvement, as well as areas that you feel quite positive about.

Setting your priorities can make a world of difference in how you live your life and what you get out of life because your actions become more personally meaningful. On the other hand, it is easy to simply make a checklist of everything you need to get done in a day and make your decisions solely based off of this list. However, when these tasks are not broken down and organized according to importance and urgency, they have no real meaning to them yet. Self-reflection and increasing self-awareness will help you with this. You will begin to feel like every decision you make is a conscious choice, rather than an action you are doing without really knowing why you are doing it. The more you are able to increase your awareness regarding your actions and decisions, the more used to intentional decision-making you will become.

In order to fully feel free to live your life on your own terms, you need to actively accept yourself. Remember that active self-acceptance doesn't mean that you don't have room to change and grow. Actually, by actively accepting yourself, you are encouraging personal growth. By fully accepting yourself, you are accepting your desire to keep growing and learning. You are constantly evolving—and this is exactly as it should be! It means that you are open to fully living in the present moment and allowing yourself to adapt to the changes necessary to be able to do so.

Active acceptance is an ongoing process. It is not something that you can work on for a few weeks, and then call it a day. Rather, it is helpful to acknowledge that there is always room for growth. Doing so means that you are actively accepting your potential—and your potential is limitless.

The more you practice active acceptance, the more satisfaction you will get out of life. Sometimes, when you feel on top of the world, it can feel as though you need to be brought down. Get rid of this thought immediately. It's okay to be unapologetically happy! It is a reflection of your commitment to living your most authentic life. It means that you are moving away from making decisions in order to fit a mold of what other people want you to be and toward shifting your focus on how you want to live your life and the person you want to be. Acting in accordance with your own values and goals is brave and vulnerable. You can be and should be the driving force behind the direction you take your life in.

Living your life unapologetically on your own terms will increase both your inward and outward clarity because you are more open to the present moment. In doing so, you will not only get rid of any lingering toxicity that you may have been holding onto, but you will also be more open to observing toxicity in others. Identifying negativity in others will allow you to move forward without letting it stand in your way or influence you to behave in ways that don't line up with how you want to live your life.

You will also begin to attract more positivity into your life, including positive people who will lift you up and encourage you, rather than bring you down with negativity or toxicity. The biggest change will come in your ability to let positive people into your life while also not letting negative people have a negative effect on you. The key lies in your belief that the opinions that toxic people have on you do not hold any leverage on you. It doesn't matter that toxic people think less of you because you are not living in accordance with how they want you to live your life; all that matters is that you are living your authentic life, whatever that may look like.

You are inherently worthy. When you start to live life on your own terms, this is an idea that you will get accustomed to. However, oftentimes we are told by society that we shouldn't feel this way about ourselves—that doing so is narcissistic. This is simply not true. You are allowed to feel proud not only of your own worth, but also of your recognition of that worth. Getting to a stage where you actively recognize your worthiness isn't as easy as it may initially sound. A lot of barriers need to be broken down along the way, which can often be a tough process, as it requires a remodeling of certain detrimental beliefs that can be very deeply ingrained within you.

It also comes with the belief that your worthiness is a part of you—that you do not need to turn to outside sources to validate your worthiness. You also do not need to prove it to others. Trying to do so not only rarely accomplishes what you want it to, but it may also be an indicator that you are still trying to get validation from other people instead of allowing active acceptance to come from within.

Everyone has inherent worth, and no one's worth is more or less than anyone else's. However, the difference lies in your ability to access your own worth. It is something that you can come back to time and time again whenever you are feeling down or want a little inspiration or confidence boost.

Remembering that no one's worth is higher than anyone else's will also help you to refrain from comparing yourself to others. Comparing yourself to others puts you in danger of equating your inherent self-worth with accomplishments. Just because the person sitting next to you has a master's degree and earns a large salary does not mean that their inherent worth is more than yours, because self-worth is not something that is determined by work, nor is it something that changes. Only the way you view your worth can change and grow, not your worth itself.

It can be beneficial to remind yourself of your self-worth from time to time. Some ways that you can easily do this include

- keeping a journal
- keeping in touch with positive people
- only using social media mindfully
- being kind to yourself
- connecting with the natural world
- cultivating gratitude
- expressing to people what you love about them

Finding affirmations that boost your self-acceptance can help remind you of your inherent self-worth as you move about your day.

- I am worthy of love.
- I am worthy of great things.
- I am capable of anything I set my mind to.
- I overcome challenges.
- I bounce back and move forward.
- I am proud of my happiness.
- I recognize my worthiness.

In order to set goals to work toward building the life you want, you must first figure out what it is you actually want from life. This involves identifying your priorities and building a clear visualization of what reaching your goals could look like. However, before you can do this, you need to allow room for authentic self-reflection. To be able to do this, you may need to shift your mindset in order to gain some clarity.

Let's say you want to be happy. This is a great start! But just saying you want to be happy does not give you any specific goals to set. While most everyone wants to be happy, getting to this place will look different for every individual because different sources bring about happiness for different people. You'll want to identify specific things that make you happy. For example, maybe spending time with your family brings you a lot of joy. This can become a priority for you. From here, you can start to make decisions that support your priority of spending time with your family. Identify what currently stands in the way of your family time. Then you can adjust the way that you are setting your priorities and making plans. In this way, you will be able to start improving your happiness by working to overcome some of the obstacles that are standing in the way of your set priority.

Take some time to reflect on your needs—which needs are being met, and which are not at the present moment. You may find that your basic human needs—things like food and shelter—are being met, while other, more complex needs are not. You can organize your needs in accordance with importance and urgency. The needs that are both important and urgent will be of the highest priority for you to address.

Your needs and your values are closely tied. Reflecting on what your individual values are will allow you to better organize your needs. When your decisions do not line up with your values, you will feel unfulfilled. It can even start to significantly take a toll on your mental health. However, when you start to take into account your values when making decisions, you will feel a stronger sense of purpose motivating your actions.

Ask yourself what you would do if you knew you would not fail. You may find that you would try a lot of new things; however, the fear of failure may be preventing you from going out and actually trying these things. Don't let fear limit you—remember that the only way to learn and grow is to try new things and to make mistakes along the way. Is there anything besides the fear of failure that is preventing you from doing these things? There may be a few practical obstacles, but usually these can be worked around. For instance, if you have always wanted to go scuba diving, but you know that before you can go on a dive, you need to spend a day completing the required training in a pool. You may be telling yourself that you can't go scuba diving because you can't find the time to do the training. This is a practical obstacle, but it is by no means a permanent obstacle. If scuba diving is something you really want to do, you will find the time to do the training. It is a matter of shifting your priorities to allow room for something you've always wanted to try.

Remember to zoom out from time to time. Zooming out allows you to see the bigger picture of your life. This can clarify what you want your life to look like. From here, you can identify certain long-term goals you want to work toward, and then break down these larger goals into more bite-sized pieces. This gives you the power to actually change the way you move through life. While the smaller goals that you set for yourself may not change your life individually, they are steps in your journey to change your life. You can remind yourself of this from time to time by recalling your zoomed-out visualization of your larger-scale goals. Make sure that the goals you are setting for yourself are in-line with the bigger-picture goal they are meant to move you toward.

You can also identify what you do not want in your life. You may find that you are allowing things you don't want in your life to take up space. Once you are able to eliminate these, you can spend time on your priorities. Set boundaries to keep negativity out of your life. This way, these negative elements will not stand in the way of your positive progress. This also has a lot to do with intentionality. Of course you will never intentionally create negative obstacles for yourself, but a lot of people do so without even realizing it. This is why self-reflection and increased self-awareness is so important. Identifying these obstacles is the first step needed to eventually tackle them.

Try different things. Sometimes the best way to approach something is with a fresh perspective. Even if you have done a certain task 100 times, try looking at it from a new point of view. This can help break you out of producing work that feels stale, and it can elevate the quality of your work tremendously. However, this will only work if you release yourself from the fear of failure. If you are afraid that something may not turn out as well as you want, you will feel more inclined to play things safe. When you accept mistakes as opportunities for growth, you will no longer feel the need to play things safe, and this is often where your best work will spring from.

The more new ways you are willing to approach something, the more you are actively rejecting perfectionism. In doing so, you are also working toward overcoming overthinking. A common source of overthinking is perfectionism. If you think about all the ways that something can go wrong because you are so set on achieving perfection, you will always try to play things as safe as possible. The irony here is that this will actually get in the way of you being able to produce more interesting and thoughtful work.

Paying attention to when you get stuck overthinking—and especially about perfectionism—will help you notice how much of your time and energy is just spent on thinking about something rather than spending time actually taking action to work toward accomplishing what you have set out to accomplish. It is in this way that overthinking so easily gets in the way of productivity. It can happen without you realizing because sometimes it can feel like the more you are thinking about a certain topic, the more you are being productive because you are considering all the ways that something could go wrong. However, this is not the case. In fact, the more you think about all the ways that something could go wrong, the more you are fortifying the wall between where you are now and the goal you want to achieve. Overthinking gets you nowhere. Release yourself from the temptation to make everything perfect because it simply will not get you to where you want to be.

Tap into your creative side to get yourself out of an overthinking cycle when it comes to perfectionism. Create some distance from the task at hand by taking a break, doing something else, and then returning to the task. You'll likely find that once you return, you feel better-equipped to solve the problem at hand because you are coming into it with a fresh perspective. You will have new thoughts surrounding the topic from taking your break, and you will be more relaxed instead of stressed about the need to solve the problem. Because of this, you will be more open to creative solutions.

Identify what your most important and urgent activities are and choose to do these activities during your peak hours. This is the time when you are able to feel the most motivated and also creative. This combination of creativity and productivity allows you the best tools to produce your most meaningful work, so it is important that you pay attention to how you are spending this time, and then make intentional decisions to tackle your priorities during this time.

Allow yourself to approach tasks nonlinearly. This is how creativity works. It activates a new part of your brain that allows you to bring something fresh to what you are doing. It allows you to make choices that you may not otherwise have made if you were to just force yourself to sit down and work straight through a certain task. This element of the unexpected is what separates creative work from uninspired work. Allow yourself a little extra time to hone your creativity, and you will find that you actually end up boosting your overall productivity.

You have all the tools needed to begin improving your life. Now it's time to use them to help you stop overthinking and get your act together!

References

Ackerman, C.E. (2017, January 18). *21 mindfulness exercises & activities for adults (+PDF)*. Positive Psychology. https://positivepsychology.com/mindfulness-exercises-techniques-activities/

Asana. (2021, November 29). *10 limiting beliefs and how to overcome them.* https://asana.com/resources/limiting-beliefs

Bailey, C. (2018, August 30). *4 strategies for overcoming distraction.* Harvard Business Review. https://hbr.org/2018/08/4-strategies-for-overcoming-distraction

Barkley, S. (2022, October 28). *Self expectations: 7 suggestions for setting realistic expectations.* PsychCentral. https://psychcentral.com/health/suggestions-for-setting-realistic-expectations-with-yourself

Boynton, E. (2021, September 15). *How to practice positive affirmations—and why they work.* Right as Rain by UW Medicine. https://rightasrain.uwmedicine.org/mind/well-being/positive-affirmations

Brandt, A. (2019, April 1). *The dangers of perfectionism.* Psychology Today. https://www.psychologytoday.com/us/blog/mindful-anger/201904/the-dangers-perfectionism

Brennan, D. (2021, October 25). *Psychological benefits of routines.* WebMD. https://www.webmd.com/mental-health/psychological-benefits-of-routine

Campbell, M. (2023, April 9). *Proven strategies for developing a good work ethic.* Growth Tactics. https://www.growthtactics.net/developing-a-good-work-ethic/

Centers for Disease Control and Prevention. (2020, April 1). *Good sleep environment.*

https://www.cdc.gov/niosh/emres/longhourstraining/environ ment.html

Chatterjee, A. (2021, September 12). *50 positive affirmations you should use daily.* ThinkRight.me. https://www.thinkrightme.com/50-positive-affirmations-you-should-use-daily/

Clark, D.A. (2014). Cognitive reconstructing. *The Wiley Handbook of Cognitive Behavioral Therapy.* 10.1002/9781118528563.wbcbt02

Cleveland Clinic. (2020, June 2). *Why downtime is essential for brain health.* https://health.clevelandclinic.org/why-downtime-is-essential-for-brain-health/

Clockify. (n.d.). *The 26 most effective time management techniques.* https://clockify.me/time-management-techniques

Cross, R., Dillon, K., & Greenberg, D. (2021, January 29). *The secret to building resilience.* Harvard Business Review. https://hbr.org/2021/01/the-secret-to-building-resilience

Cuncic, A. (2023, February 13). *Negative thoughts: How to stop them.* VeryWell Mind. https://www.verywellmind.com/how-to-change-negative-thinking-3024843

Dizon, P. (2023, February 23). *Overcoming procrastination: Strategies for staying focused and getting things done.* Taskable. https://taskablehq.com/blog/overcoming-procrastination-strategies-for-staying-focused-and-getting-things-done

Fletcher, J. (2022, June 16). *How to practice mindful listening.* PsychCentral. https://psychcentral.com/lib/mindful-listening-exercise

Fowler, P. (2022, January 17). *Breathing techniques for stress relief.* WebMD. https://www.webmd.com/balance/stress-management/stress-relief-breathing-techniques

Hagan, E. (2021, February 14). *The power of self-love and self-compassion.* Psychology Today. https://www.psychologytoday.com/us/blog/being-your-best-self/202102/the-power-self-love-and-self-compassion

Harvard Health Publishing. (2020, October 1). *Tips to improve concentration.* https://www.health.harvard.edu/mind-and-mood/tips-to-improve-concentration

Harvard School of Public Health. (n.d.). *Sleep.* https://www.hsph.harvard.edu/nutritionsource/sleep/

Herrity, J. (2022, September 30). *8 helpful strategies for conflict management.* Indeed. https://www.indeed.com/career-advice/career-development/strategies-for-conflict-management

Heshmat, S. (2017, March 25). *10 strategies for developing self-control.* Psychology Today. https://www.psychologytoday.com/us/blog/science-choice/201703/10-strategies-developing-self-control

Hirschlag, A. (2022, June 2). *Do you live with anxiety? Here are 13 ways to cope.* Healthline. https://www.healthline.com/health/mental-health/how-to-cope-with-anxiety

Humphreys, A. (n.d.). *Strategies for embracing challenges.* Rack Up Moments. https://rackupmoments.com/strategies-for-embracing-challenges/

Indeed Editorial Team. (2022a, June 24). *How to break down tasks in 5 steps (plus tips).* Indeed. https://www.indeed.com/career-advice/career-development/how-to-break-down-tasks

Indeed Editorial Team. (2022b, June 24). *Time management goals to take control of your time (with examples).* Indeed. https://www.indeed.com/career-advice/career-development/time-management-goals

Indeed Editorial Team. (2022c, July 5). *How to set realistic goals.* Indeed. https://www.indeed.com/career-advice/career-development/how-to-set-realistic-goals

Indeed Editorial Team. (2023, February 3). *How to set priorities in 4 steps (plus effective strategies).* Indeed. https://www.indeed.com/career-advice/career-development/how-to-set-priorities

Ishak, R. (2023, April 25). *50 positive affirmations that will change your life*. The Everygirl. https://theeverygirl.com/50-positive-affirmations-you-should-tell-yourself/

Kabrick, S. (2021, July 20). *11 tips for coping with an anxiety disorder*. Mayo Clinic Health System. https://www.mayoclinichealthsystem.org/hometown-health/speaking-of-health/11-tips-for-coping-with-an-anxiety-disorder

Kamau, C. (2022, October). *Visualization meditation: Benefits and techniques to help you unlock the life of your dreams*. BetterMe. https://betterme.world/articles/visualization-meditation/

Knight, R. (2019, April 29). *How to manage your perfectionism*. Harvard Business Review. https://hbr.org/2019/04/how-to-manage-your-perfectionism

Kohll, A. (2018, May 29). New study shows correlation between employee engagement and the long-lost lunch break. *Forbes*. https://www.forbes.com/sites/alankohll/2018/05/29/new-study-shows-correlation-between-employee-engagement-and-the-long-lost-lunch-break/?sh=74b7a80d4efc

Lamothe, C. (2023, February 15). *14 ways to stop overthinking*. Healthline. https://www.healthline.com/health/how-to-stop-overthinking

Lant, K. (2018, February 20). 5 ways to grow your creativity and productivity at the same time. *Fast Company*. https://www.fastcompany.com/40532541/5-ways-to-grow-your-creativity-and-productivity-at-the-same-time

Li, L. (2020, April 22). *10 ways to meet your goals with time management*. TinyPulse. https://www.tinypulse.com/blog/10-ways-to-meet-your-goals-with-time-management

Lidford, P. (2018, July). *5 coaching techniques to break free from limiting beliefs*. The Coaching Academy. https://www.the-coaching-academy.com/blog/2018/07/3026

Lindberg, S. (2022, October 21). *Need help staying focused? Try these 10 tips.* Healthline. https://www.healthline.com/health/mental-health/how-to-stay-focused

Linscott, M. (2023, January 20). *How to be SMART about goal-setting.* Purdue University Global. https://purdueglobalwriting.center/2023/01/20/how-to-be-smart-about-goal-setting/

Lopez, A. (2023, February 28). *10 effective strategies for building self-discipline and willpower.* You Just Try. https://www.ujusttry.com/building-self-discipline-and-willpower/

Lucia, G. (2021, July 22). *Why do people overthink and what causes overthinking?* Limit Breaker. https://limitbreaker.co/why-do-people-overthink-and-what-causes-overthinking/

Luke, C. (2020). *What is overthinking: Causes and effects.* Budding Psychologists. https://buddingpsychologists.org/what-is-overthinking-causes-and-effects/

Making Caring Common Project. (2021, March). *5 tips for cultivating empathy.* Harvard Graduate School of Education. https://mcc.gse.harvard.edu/resources-for-families/5-tips-cultivating-empathy

Manning, J.M. (2020). Goal setting and self-discipline. In *The Path to Building a Successful Nursing Career.* Springer, Cham. https://doi.org/10.1007/978-3-030-50023-8_2

MantraCare. (n.d.). *Negative self talk: Strategies to break the cycle of negativity.* https://mantracare.org/therapy/self-care/negative-self-talk/

Maps, I.R. (2016, November 11). *How to boost your wellbeing—the benefits of a growth mindset.* Psychlopaedia. https://psychlopaedia.org/learning-and-development/how-to-boost-your-wellbeing-the-benefits-of-a-growth-mindset/

Martins, J. (2022, December 16). *18 time management tips, strategies, and quick wins to get your best work done.* Asana. https://asana.com/resources/time-management-tips

Maximets, N. (2021, December 10). *8 ways to develop self-discipline and improve willpower*. Inside of Happiness. https://insideofhappiness.com/ways-to-develop-self-discipline-and-improve-willpower/

Mayo Clinic. (2022a, February 3). *Positive thinking: Stop negative self-talk to reduce stress*. https://www.mayoclinic.org/healthy-lifestyle/stress-management/in-depth/positive-thinking/art-20043950

Mayo Clinic. (2022b, April 28). *Relaxation techniques: Try these steps to reduce stress*. https://www.mayoclinic.org/healthy-lifestyle/stress-management/in-depth/relaxation-technique/art-20045368

Mayo Clinic. (2022c, April 29). *Meditation: A simple, fast way to reduce stress*. https://www.mayoclinic.org/tests-procedures/meditation/in-depth/meditation/art-20045858

Mayo Clinic. (2022d, May 7). *Sleep tips: 6 steps to better sleep*. https://www.mayoclinic.org/healthy-lifestyle/adult-health/in-depth/sleep/art-20048379

Mayo Clinic. (2022e, October 11). *Mindfulness exercises*. https://www.mayoclinic.org/healthy-lifestyle/consumer-health/in-depth/mindfulness-exercises/art-20046356

Mello Woman. (2023, May 2). *Is overthinking sabotaging your productivity?* https://mellowoman.com/overthinking-affecting-productivity/

Mindful Focused. (n.d.). *5 simple strategies for overcoming procrastination and boosting productivity*. https://mindfulfocused.com/5-simple-strategies-for-overcoming-procrastination-and-boosting-productivity/

Monae, A. (2023, March 23). 6 things you gain by embracing failure and learning from mistakes. *Entrepreneur*. https://www.entrepreneur.com/growing-a-business/6-things-you-gain-by-embracing-failure/447404

Moore, C. (2019, June 2). *How to practice self-compassion: 8 techniques and tips*. Positive Psychology.

https://positivepsychology.com/how-to-practice-self-compassion/

Morin, A. (2023, February 14). *How to stop overthinking: Here's how to recognize the signs that you're overthinking.* VeryWell Mind. https://www.verywellmind.com/how-to-know-when-youre-overthinking-5077069

Mulla, R. (2021, December 6). *Can't sleep? Overthinking? How thought blocking can help.* Sleepstation. https://www.sleepstation.org.uk/articles/sleep-tips/thought-blocking/

Muthoni, J. (2023, January 30). *Finding inspiration from failure: Why it's important to view mistakes as learning opportunities.* Jonas Muthoni. https://jonasmuthoni.com/finding-inspiration-from-failure-why-its-important-to-view-mistakes-as-learning-opportunities/

National Sleep Foundation. (2020, November 12). *The link between nutrition and sleep.* https://www.thensf.org/the-link-between-nutrition-and-sleep/

NHS. (2022, September 14). *Mindfulness.* https://www.nhs.uk/mental-health/self-help/tips-and-support/mindfulness/

Northwestern Medicine. (2022, December). *Health benefits of having a routine: Tips for a healthier lifestyle.* https://www.nm.org/healthbeat/healthy-tips/health-benefits-of-having-a-routine

O'Connell, V.A. (2014, August 14). The healthy college student: The impact of daily routines on illness burden. *SAGE Open, 4*(3). https://doi.org/10.1177/2158244014547181

Oppland, M. (2017, April 28). *13 most popular gratitude exercises & activities.* Positive Psychology. https://positivepsychology.com/gratitude-exercises/

Pace, R. (2022, July 4). *How to build empathy in relationships.* Marriage.com. https://www.marriage.com/advice/relationship/how-to-build-empathy-in-relationships/

Pettit, M. (2020, June 26). *6 ways to develop a gratitude mindset.* Lucemi Consulting. https://lucemiconsulting.co.uk/gratitude-mindset/

Positive Miracle. (2022, March 23). *What are the advantages and disadvantages of having a growth mindset?* https://positivemiracle.com/advantages-disadvantages-growth-mindset/

Psychology Today. (n.d.). *Perfectionism.* https://www.psychologytoday.com/us/basics/perfectionism

Pugle, M. (2021, September 15). *Chronic stress can lead to higher blood pressure: Here's how to reduce it.* Healthline. https://www.healthline.com/health-news/chronic-stress-can-lead-to-higher-blood-pressure-heres-how-to-reduce-it

Reisenwitz, C. (n.d.). *7 life-changing benefits of daily routines.* Clockwise. https://www.getclockwise.com/blog/benefits-daily-routines

Rice, A. (2021, September 13). *How to challenge negative self-talk.* PsychCentral. https://psychcentral.com/lib/challenging-negative-self-talk

Richards, L. (2022, March 18). *What is positive self-talk?* Medical News Today. https://www.medicalnewstoday.com/articles/positive-self-talk

Robbins, T. (n.d.). *How to overcome self-doubt.* Tony Robbins. https://www.tonyrobbins.com/mental-health/how-to-overcome-self-doubt/

Ruggeri, A. (2018, February 20). *The dangerous downsides of perfectionism.* BBC Future. https://www.bbc.com/future/article/20180219-toxic-perfectionism-is-on-the-rise

Samuel, A. (2021, March 3). *Taking a break doesn't always mean unplugging.* Harvard Business Review. https://hbr.org/2021/03/taking-a-break-doesnt-always-mean-unplugging

Santilli, M. (2023, March 10). How to stop overthinking: Causes and ways to cope. *Forbes Health.*

https://www.forbes.com/health/mind/what-causes-overthinking-and-6-ways-to-stop/

Sasson, R. (n.d.). *Self discipline benefits and its importance in your life.* Success Consciousness. https://www.successconsciousness.com/blog/inner-strength/self-discipline/

Schroeder, B. (2019, July 12). 12 advantages of a growth mindset that could accelerate your career. *Forbes.* https://www.forbes.com/sites/bernhardschroeder/2019/07/12/12-advantages-of-a-growth-mindset-that-could-accelerate-your-career/?sh=6658510013f4

Scott, E. (2020, July 1). *How to reduce stress with breathing exercises.* VeryWell Mind. https://www.verywellmind.com/how-to-reduce-stress-with-breathing-exercises-3144508

Scott, E. (2022, May 24). *The toxic effects of negative self-talk.* VeryWell Mind. https://www.verywellmind.com/negative-self-talk-and-how-it-affects-us-4161304

Selva, J. (2018, March 8). *What is Albert Ellis' ABC Model in CBT Theory? (Incl. PDF).* Positive Psychology. https://positivepsychology.com/albert-ellis-abc-model-rebt-cbt/

Sheldon, R. &Wigmore, I. (2022, September 15). *Pomodoro technique.* Tech Target. https://www.techtarget.com/whatis/definition/pomodoro-technique

Skills You Need. (n.d.). *Mindful listening.* Skills You Need. https://www.skillsyouneed.com/ips/mindful-listening.html

Smith, S. (2022, December 28). *How to handle overthinking in a relationship.* Marriage.com. https://www.marriage.com/advice/relationship/is-overthinking-in-a-relationship-bad-for-you/

Smith Breon, A. (2021, November 9). *How to cultivate a gratitude practice.* Johns Hopkins University. https://wellbeing.jhu.edu/blog/2021/11/09/how-to-cultivate-a-gratitude-practice/

Suni, E. (2023a, March 17). *Nutrition and sleep.* Sleep Foundation.
https://www.sleepfoundation.org/nutrition

Suni, E. (2023b, April 17). *Anxiety and sleep.* Sleep Foundation.
https://www.sleepfoundation.org/mental-health/anxiety-and-sleep

Suni, E. (2023c, May 5). *How to design the ideal bedroom for sleep.* Sleep
Foundation. https://www.sleepfoundation.org/bedroom-environment/how-to-design-the-ideal-bedroom-for-sleep

Sutton, J. (2021, December 20). *7 stress-relief breathing exercises for
calming your mind.* Positive Psychology.
https://positivepsychology.com/breathing-exercises-for-stress-relief/

The Happy Manager. (n.d.). *20 tips to reduce time wasters.* https://the-happy-manager.com/tip/time-wasters/

The Supplement Co. (n.d.). *Tips for improving sleep quality and
quantity.* https://thesupplementco.com/blogs/news/tips-for-improving-sleep-quality-and-quantity

Thibault, I. (2023, March 9). *Why you should embrace failure and make
it your ally.* Medium.
https://medium.com/@ikethibault/embracing-failure-for-personal-growth-strategies-and-benefits-6c5a55b442ae

Timeular. (2022, November 25). *How to set realistic goals: The ultimate
guide to achieve them.* https://timeular.com/blog/how-set-realistic-goals/

UGA Today. (2014, March 24). *Break large tasks down into more
manageable pieces.* University of Georgia.
https://news.uga.edu/break-large-tasks-down-into-smaller-more-manageable-pieces/

Vadlamani, S. (n.d.). *Embrace imperfection: Six ways to celebrate your
flaws.* Happiness.
https://www.happiness.com/magazine/personal-growth/embrace-your-imperfections/

Virtues for Life. (n.d.). *50 affirmations to help you make positive change.* https://www.virtuesforlife.com/50-affirmations-to-help-you-make-positive-change/

Wilding, M. (2021, February 10). *How to stop overthinking everything.* Harvard Business Review. https://hbr.org/2021/02/how-to-stop-overthinking-everything

Wisner, W. (2023, January 26). *25 positive daily affirmations to recite for your mental health.* VeryWell Mind. https://www.verywellmind.com/positive-daily-affirmations-7097067

Yasmine, A. (2021). *50 daily affirmations to improve your life.* Ariel Yasmine. https://arielyasmine.com/daily-affirmations/

Yugay, I. (2018, February 13). *How to develop the self-discipline needed to achieve your goals.* Mindvalley. https://blog.mindvalley.com/self-discipline/

Images

Content Pixie. (2020). *Woman in white button up shirt holding white braille paper photo* [Photo]. Unsplash. https://unsplash.com/photos/uxEH3TufYNU

Duke, J. (2021). *A woman is doing exercises on a yoga mat photo* [Photo]. Unsplash. https://unsplash.com/photos/_PInKGPLPCA

Heftiba, T. (2017). *White printer paper photo* [Photo]. Unsplash. https://unsplash.com/photos/yz4VF6x0W3M

Janssens, E. (2017). *White ceramic mug with coffee on top of a planner photo* [Photo]. Unsplash. https://unsplash.com/photos/aQfhbxailCs

Lopes, H. (2017). *Four person hands wrap around shoulders while looking at sunset photo* [Photo]. Unsplash. https://unsplash.com/photos/PGnqT0rXWLs

Rae, S. (2018). *Person holding bell pepper photo* [Photo]. Unsplash. https://unsplash.com/photos/t4XYbj1q_Cc

Turner, T. (2020). *Women in red and white floral dress painting photo* [Photo]. Unsplash. https://unsplash.com/photos/QrYt4_K5TIc

Visual Design. (2020). *Macbook pro on brown wooden table photo* [Photo]. Unsplash. https://unsplash.com/photos/_rhsR_CVw9U

Volant. (2021). *A woman in black sports bra top sitting in a yoga pose photo* [Photo]. Unsplash. https://unsplash.com/photos/_2NYDijyewY

Wocintechchat. (2019). *Two women sitting beside table and talking photo* [Photo]. Unsplash. https://unsplash.com/photos/LQ1t-8Ms5PY

Printed in Great Britain
by Amazon